COMPANION
TO THE
HIGH HOLYDAYS PRAYER BOOK

Ha'rav Lord Jakobovits זצ"ל

COMPANION to the HIGH HOLYDAYS PRAYER BOOK
מחזור

HA'RAV LORD JAKOBOVITS זצ"ל
Emeritus Chief Rabbi

Reuben Turner
Editorial Co-ordinator

VALLENTINE MITCHELL
LONDON • PORTLAND, OR

First Published in 2002 in Great Britain by
VALLENTINE MITCHELL
Crown House, 47 Chase Side,
Southgate, London N14 5BP

and in the United States of America by
VALLENTINE MITCHELL
c/o ISBS
5804 N.E. Hassalo Street
Portland, Oregan 97213-3644

Website http://www.vmbooks.com

Copyright @ 2002 Lord Jakobovits

British Library Cataloguing in Publication Data:

A catalogue record for this book is availabe from the British Library

ISBN 0 85303 434 6 (paper)

Jakobovits, Ha'Rav Lord
  Companion to the High Holydays prayer book
  1. High Holidays
  I. Title II. Turner, Reuben, 1924–
  296.4'31

Library of Congress Cataloging-in-Publication Data:

Jakobovits, Immanuel, Sir, 1921–
  Companion to the High Holydays prayer book [mahazor] / by Lord Jakobovits.
    p. cm.
  Compiled by Reuben Turner.
  ISBN 0-85303-434-6 (pbk.)
  1. High Holidays. 2. Maòzor. High Holidays. 3. Prayer–Judaism. 4. High Holiday sermons. 5. Jewish sermons, English. I. Turner, Rueben. II. Title.
BM693.H5 J35 2001
296.4'31–dc21

2001052211

All rights reserved. No part of this publication may be reproduced, stored in or introduced into a retrieval system or transmitted in any form or by any means, electronic, mechanical, photocopying, recording or otherwise, without the prior written permission of the publisher of this book.

Typeset by Cambridge Photosetting Services
in 11/14 pt Garamond

Printed in Great Britain by MPG Books Ltd, Bodmin, Cornwall

Contents

Preface by Rev. Reuben Turner viii
Foreword by Chief Rabbi Sacks ix
Tribute by Graham Aaronson QC xi
Letter from Chief Rabbi Israel Meir Lau xiii

I. **Rosh Hashanah**

    The Distinction of the Days of Awe among the Festivals 3
    Rosh Hashanah and Yom Kippur: Two Facets of Repentence 4
    Rosh Hashanah: The Name 5
    Three Names 7
    The Season 8
        Nature's Challenge to Man 9
    Anniversary of Creation 11
        Evolution and the Uniqueness of Man 13
    The Jewish Idea of Prayer 14
        Self-improvement through Prayer 15
    The Atmosphere of Prayer 17
        How Can God 'Dwell' in Synagogues? 17
    Devotion at Prayer 19
        Modern Man's Lost Art of Prayer 20
        Operating on the Heart 22
        Ten Ways of Enhancing Kavanah 23
    Praying with a Congregation 25
        Swaying during Prayer and Study 28
        The Virtue of Congregational Prayer 28
    The Rosh Hashanah and Yom Kippur Texts and Commentaries 29
    A Short Survey of Machzor Commentaries and English Translations 32
    Rites, Translations and English Editions 34

Some Machzor Themes 37
Biblical Readings for Rosh Hashanah 39
Three Women Heading the New Year 42
Products of Prayer 43
Sarah – The More Perceptive Parent 44
Yitzchak – He shall have the Last Laugh 44
First Day Rosh Hashanah – The Origins of the
Jewish People 45
Second Day Rosh Hashanah – The Sacrifice of
Isaac 46
Haftorah for First Day Rosh Hashanah –
Hannah's Prayer 47
Haftarah for Second Day Rosh Hashanah –
Rachel: Mother of Comfort and National Return 49
The Role of Women 51
Man and Women in the Scheme of Creation 52
All Mankind United 52

II. **Sermons**
   Rosh Hashanah
   1. The Blessings of Fear 57
   2. 'With All Thine Heart' – The Meaning of Prayer 64
   3. The Human Rights Revolution 71
   4. 'For Man is Born to Labour' 79
   5. The Scientific Revolution 83
   Yom Kippur
   1. 'With All Thy Mind' – Our Belief in God 89
   2. 'The Religious Revolution 99
   3. The Burdens of the Rabbi's Labour 108
   Yizkor
   1. Reflections on the Jewish Concept of
      After-life 118
   2. 'With All Thy Might' – Ethics and Religion 125
   3. The Moral Revolution 130

Musaph
  1. Collective Labour 139
  2. Farewell to my Congregation 146
      The Three Functions of a Congregation 147
      The Testimony of a Congregation 148
      The Rabbi as Teacher 149
      The Togetherness of a Congregation 150
      The Rabbi as Head 151
      The Individuals of a Congregation 152
      The Rabbi as Agent 152
Ne'ilah
  1. The Pangs of Labour 154
  2. Leaving in Peace 158

III. **Broadcasts** 167
  1. Creation and Judgement 167
  2. Reaching the Moon: Two Perspectives 173
  3. The Meaning of Prayer and Confession 179

בע״ה

Preface

The qualities of Aaron the High Priest: 'Humility, uprightness and integrity,' can justly be attributed to the author of this *Companion*: a distinguished-looking figure and internationally recognized Torah scholar, teacher, thinker, preacher and innovator; great in stature, yet humble in nature. The wish of Ha'Rav Jakobovits זצ״ל was to write a commentary on the High Holydays Machzor as an introduction to each section of the Rosh Hashanah and Yom Kippur Prayer Book. Alas, the Emeritus Chief Rabbi passed away in the middle of his work. However, it was felt that with the inclusion of sermons and broadcasts, the publication would serve as a permanent literary memorial to a true giant in Jewish thought and originality. These original thoughts and perceptions should promote discussion and elaboration on themes that are timeless and at the same time as relevant today as they were in the past.

Having had the *Zechut* and privilege to put together this *Companion*, I pray that the Rav זצ״ל will be a *meilitz yosher* for the whole of *K'lal Yisrael*.

Reuben Turner

Marcheshvan 5762/October 2001

Foreword

Throughout his life, Lord Jakobovits of blessed memory זצ"ל held a project close to his heart. He wanted to write a commentary to the prayers of the High Holidays. The sheer pressure of his work as Chief Rabbi kept him from completing it, though he would turn to it from time to time and set down his ideas; and it is these that have now been published in the present work.

Lord Jakobovits loved the liturgy of Rosh Hashanah and Yom Kippur. There is an old hassidic story of the young disciple who came to the Rebbe and said, 'I have been through the whole of the Talmud.' The Rebbe gently asked: 'You have been through the whole of the Talmud. But how much of the Talmud has been through you?' Lord Jakobovits had done more than go through the prayers. They had gone through him. They became part of his vocabulary, his way of speaking about the world. I remember visiting a school in Sydney, Australia, and seeing the inscription he had written in the visitors' book many years before. He had written *Ashrei ayin ra'ata kol eleh*, 'Happy is the eye that has seen all these things' – a quotation from the Musaf of Yom Kippur. Frequently in our conversations over the years he would use a phrase from the High Holy Days' liturgy. It was clear to me that he regarded these prayers as part of the lexicon of Jewish sensibility. He loved them, internalised them, and wove them into his words.

His insights into Jewish texts were always arresting, and it is a great shame that he was unable to set them all down. He knew, though, as well as anyone the depth of Rabbi Tarfon's insight that: 'It is not yours to complete the work, but neither are you free to desist from it.' He lived by that principle and we are the heirs to his great achievements in many fields, not least that of

Torah scholarship. These notes and commentaries will enhance our understanding of the structure and detail of Jewish prayer and will stand as a memorial to one who did more than most to 'make Torah great and glorious' in our time.

Jonathan Sacks

Chief Rabbi Professor Jonathan Sacks

Erev Sukkot 5762/October 2001

Tribute

For many years I have felt a degree of frustration at the shallowness of my understanding of the Rosh Hashanah and Yom Kippur services. The ancient liturgy, however beautiful its expression and however sensitive its translation, frequently hides its meaning and true significance from unscholarly congregants like myself. I wondered whether someone had written a commentary that would help me to gain a deeper understanding of the prayers and, indeed, of the significance of these holy days.

I mentioned this to Rabbi Dr Jeffrey Cohen of Stanmore and Canons Park Synagogue. He told me that Lord Jakobovits had intended to write such a commentary, and suggested that I should contact him. This was three years ago.

When I met Lord Jakobovits I was overwhelmed by his enthusiasm for the project. He had already written a substantial body of commentaries and immediately offered to do everything he could to help produce the finished work. I left the meeting with a bundle of manuscripts and a determination to do what little I could to help the project reach fruition: the completion and publication of his commentaries would be an ideal way of offering laymen like myself an insight into our prayers.

The news of Lord Jakobovits' death two years ago came as a terrible shock. I had been given the privilege of working with him, and rapidly come to appreciate what a remarkable man he was – a great scholar, of course, but also full of warmth and kindness. And it was the warmth and kindness that Amelie, Lady Jakobovits, continued to show me and my wife Pearl that made me all the more determined to make sure that the commentaries were published.

Last week I brought the page-proofs of the commentaries to synagogue. Their beautiful prose seemed to accord well with the tone of the prayers, while their constant insights made the service much more meaningful. With real satisfaction I noted that my friends sitting nearby were equally absorbed and moved by the pages that I passed to them. It was apparent that the commentaries had achieved their aim of providing insight and meaning to the services, and in a style that was a pleasure to read.

It is so sad that Lord Jakobovits did not live to see the publication of these commentaries. It has been my privilege to play a small part in bringing them to publication, and in this way to enable a wider congregation to enjoy the benefit of his immense scholarship and humanity.

Graham Aaronson

October 2001

> The publishers are grateful to Mr Graham Aaronson, QC, for his generosity in making the publication of this book possible.

ISRAEL MEIR LAU
Chief Rabbi of Israel
President of The Great Rabbinical Court

ישראל מאיר לאו
הרב הראשי לישראל
נשיא בית הדין הרבני הגדול

ב"ז Tishrei תשס"ב
October 14, 2001
R-82-01

Rabbi Shmuel Jakobovitz
Jerusalem

Dear Rabbi Shmuel Jakobovitz :

I have heard of your intention to publish the Torah writings and thoughts of your late father, Chief Rabbi of the British Commonwealth, Lord Emanuel Jakobovitz zt"l, whose personality personified the Kingdom of Torah. His noble personality and manner of living influenced many throughout Great Britain and molded the English Jewish Religious life, as we know it today.

Many of the previous works of the Chief Rabbi dealt primarily with the topic of Medicine in Halacha. His works served as a basis for many who later wished to expand on this complex topic.

I saw the new work "A Companion to the Machzor" which your late father zt"l began to write in his lifetime, now to be published. The concepts are presented in a clear and cultured manner emphasizing the uniqueness of Torah and Jewish Holidays.

I have no doubt that this is a great undertaking. By continuing to spread the life of his teachings we are once again immortalizing his image. May his memory be blessed.

Sincerely Yours ,

Israel Meir Lau
ISRAEL MEIR LAU
CHIEF RABBI OF ISRAEL

ראש השנה

ROSH HASHANAH

I
Rosh Hashanah

The Distinction of the Days of Awe among the Festivals

Rosh Hashanah and Yom Kippur belong to the annual cycle of the five festivals listed in the Torah in chronological order – Pesach, Shavu'ot, Rosh Hashanah, Yom Kippur and Succot (Lev. 23 and Num. 28). There are three further listings of the Festivals (Ex. 23 and 34; and Deut. 16). But these listings omit Rosh Hashanah and Yom Kippur, mentioning only the three Pilgrim Festivals which alone are pastoral or agricultural in character. Moreover, they stress the social significance of the Festivals (to rejoice with your family as well as the poor and the stranger). Rosh Hashanah and Yom Kippur have no such seasonal or social significance.

This distinction leads to a striking contrast. The familiar commandment, 'Three times a year shall all your males appear before the Lord your God' in the Temple in Jerusalem is repeated several times in the Torah. An uninitiated reader might suspect that such appearance before God, three times a year, could possible refer to the three-times-a-year synagogue visits by some Jews on the two days of Rosh Hashanah and on Yom Kippur, whereas the reference is, of course, to the three 'Foot Festivals' of Pesach, Shavu'ot and Succot which demanded visits to the Temple site in Jerusalem. Not so Rosh Hashanah and Yom Kippur which required no such pilgrimage. And yet one would surely assume that because the Days of Awe are intended as more intensive and stirring religious experiences than the three Pilgrim Festivals, it would be mandatory for them to be celebrated within the solemnity of Jerusalem.

In fact, it is this very anomaly which highlights the special significance of the High Festivals. On other festive occasions, as it were, *it is we who have to go to God*, for the fullest expression of their spirit can be found only in Jerusalem and its Temple. On Rosh Hashanah and Yom Kippur, however, *God comes to us*, and we are to experience His Presence wherever we are. 'Seek the Lord while He may be found, call upon Him while He is near' (Is. 55:6), say our Sages, refers to the Ten Days of Penitence. A Jew who does not sense the proximity of God at this season has not understood its message and has failed in his devotions.

Rosh Hashanah and Yom Kippur: Two Facets of Repentance

During the penitential season we look back over the year gone by and we look forward to the new year just beginning. The process of repentance embraces both aspects. Maimonides, followed by most other leading authorities, lists the following three essential ingredients in true repentance: *confession* of sins; *regret* that they were ever committed; and the *resolve* to eliminate these lapses in the future.

This two-directional aspect of repentance is reflected in the principal difference between Rosh Hashanah and Yom Kippur. Rosh Hashanah, at the *head* or the beginning of the year, focuses on the New Year which the Festival inaugurates. Shakespeare may assert 'All's well that ends well'; Judaism maintains all is well that *begins* well. Therefore every beginning is to be consecrated. The first-born among men and animals, the first-fruits among plants, as indeed the first days of a new year – all belong to God. They are to be offered to the priests as His agents, or brought to His Temple, or specially sanctified in the synagogue – on the assumption that if the first or the beginning is elevated, the rest will follow suit: we consecrate the first-born as holy so that other children will follow the example; we treat the first-fruits as sacred, so that the blessing of the entire harvest will be seen as a gift of God; and we anticipate that all the days of the year will draw their inspiration from the uplifting Days of Awe at the beginning of the new year.

For this reason, there is no recital of confession of sins on Rosh Hashanah. Sin has no part in the resolutions for the year ahead. The New Year is not a review; it is, rather, a preview.

The charge to look back belongs primarily to Yom Kippur. It seeks atonement for past offences. Its main theme is the quest for forgiveness for wrongs committed during the year gone by.

Our Sages, with their impressive homiletical insight, expressed this distinction in their interpretation of the opening words of Psalm 27 recited daily at this season: 'The Lord is my light and my salvation – "My light" refers to Rosh Hashanah; and "My salvation", that refers to Yom Kippur'. A light serves only to illuminate the way ahead, the forward path, not the one already traversed. Salvation, on the other hand, refers to rescue or redemption from a state of past danger or imperfection.

Of these two elements which constitute repentance – looking forward and backward – precedence is given to the future. It is Rosh Hashanah which comes before Yom Kippur, heralding the New Year. Perhaps even more significantly, the entire Ten Days of Penitence occur not at the end of the year gone by but at the beginning of the new year yet to come; the start and not the finish of the year is especially hallowed. Penitence belongs to the future more than to the past!

Rosh Hashanah: The Name

Both Hebrew words used to describe the Festival stand for essential features of it. We speak not of a 'New Year' but literally of the 'Head of the Year'.

The head is the seat of the intellect and the nerve-centre from which go out commands and controls to all parts of the body. In the same way Rosh Hashanah is to *head* the entire year; one's thoughts and movements throughout the year are to be governed by the inspiration of Rosh Hashanah.

The second word, *Hashanah*, is likewise most instructive. *Shanah*, meaning 'year', comes from a root which means both 'to repeat' and 'to change'. Thus, derivatives from the first meaning are common words like *shenayim*, *mishneh*, and *veshinantam*, meaning 'two', 'study by repetition' (as in *Mishneh Torah* – Deuteronomy, and the *Mishnah* of the Talmud), and 'you shall learn diligently' in the *Shema*. On the one hand, then, the year represents a cycle which 'repeats' itself annually, just as real learning is repeating what one has learnt.

But the same root, as in *meshaneh* or *shinui*, also connotes 'alter' or 'change'. No new year is meant to be identical with the one gone by. If we are the same this year as the year before, and one Rosh Hashanah is merely a 'repeat' of the previous one, life has little or no meaning, for it remains woefully and wastefully at a standstill.

Judaism is a combination of ideals which stay inviolate, changeless, immutable, with the dynamics of flexibility and constant 'change'. innovation and adjustment to new conditions. It is this balance between the old and the new, between the timely and the timeless, which characterizes the capacity of Judaism to remain, rocklike, impervious to the waves and tides of all ages, and yet to respond with fresh insights as a leading progressive force in a world filled with a restless human condition as man ceaselessly quests to expand the boundaries of knowledge and creativeness.

Jewish law itself reflects this balance or contrast between the static and the dynamic. The practice of Judaism is commonly known as *halachah* from the Hebrew *halach* – 'to go' or 'to walk'. Characteristically, the Torah declares: 'If you will *walk* in My statutes...' (Lev. 26:3). One walks along a path. Its width is determined, and the moment one strays from it, one 'departs' from the right way. But its length is indeterminate, and one moves constantly forward towards one's destination. In one sense, Jewish law is strictly circumscribed and immutable; in another, it forever advances as it develops in response to new challenges in every age.

Each Rosh Hashanah is to be treated as another landmark on the passage through life, representing on the one hand the continuity of 'repeating' ageless traditions, and on the other, of 'changing' and developing as circumstances change and demand ever-new responses in the light of fixed values.

Judaism charges us, in the felicitous words of Rav Kook, 'to renew the old and to sanctify the new'.

There is of course a difference between what is static and what is subject to change. Judaism, it has been said, will never be in accordance with the times until the times are in accordance with Judaism (S.R. Hirsch). What is constant in Rosh Hashanah predominates over what may alter from year to year.

Three Names

The Festival is known by three entirely different names, originating in three separate epochs of Jewish history. The *biblical* name is *Yom Teru'ah* – 'Day of the Blowing of the Shofar' (Num. 29:1). *Rosh Hashanah* itself is the *talmudic* name, used as the title of the tractate dealing with the Festival. (In the Tenach, Rosh Hashanah occurs only incidentally in Ez. 40:1, where it is used to denote the Tenth of Tishri, i.e. the day of Yom Kippur.)

The *liturgical* name, used in all our statutory prayers, is *Yom Hazikaron* – 'Day of Remembrance', man's 'birthday', when God 'remembers' all humans He created and judges them.

These three names correspond to the three major sections of the *Musaph Amidah: Rosh* Hashanah, as the 'Head' of the year, parallels *Malchuyot* – the proclamation of God's 'Kingship' or '*Head*ship'.

Yom Hazikaron is represented by the section called *Zichronot*, which affirms that God remembers 'all whom He created' and judges their deeds.

Finally, *Yom Teru'ah* corresponds to the last section, *Shofarot*, the passages dealing with episodes in Jewish history (particularly the Revelation at Sinai) when the Shofar was sounded and which will be blown to herald the Final Redemption.

The Season

While Rosh Hashanah is not a seasonal Festival in the manner in which Pesach, Shavu'ot and Succot celebrate the Spring, the Harvest, and the Ingathering of the Fruits, its fixture at the autumn is of moral significance.

This is the time of the year when everything cyclical reaches its perfection, calling on man not to lag behind the lower forms of life. How much more so must man, as the crown of creation endowed with intellect, seek to reach perfection before his Creator at this season, lest he be surpassed by the lower creatures?!

This idea is magnificently presented by Samson Raphael Hirsch. The thought is so stirring and its expression so poetic, that it merits quoting verbatim (in translation).

NATURE'S CHALLENGE TO MAN

The summer is drawing to a close. The earth receives the final glow of the sun and its fruits approach their full maturity. Everything that grows and lives seeks to extract the maximum of ripeness from the last rays of the year. The apple paints itself with its final shade of red, the wine receives its richest sparkle. The ground gives its last sap, the corn-stalks grow to their limit. The bee seeks the last drop of honey in the flower cup before it vanishes. The squirrel drags the last grain of corn to his winter store. The returning swallow carries the last straw to the nest. There is no time to be lost; the end is in sight. The Master will soon call. Everything seeks while there is still time to attain and to achieve the best that is in it. It does not wish to appear before its Master with fragmentary and half-finished work, with its year's performance still defective...

All things strive to go straight, every being, every power, every dynamic atom. They all have their eye on the goal which has been fixed for them, and endeavour to reach it by the most direct way, resolute, sharp, strong and firm, with no deviation or circuit. Is it only the way of man which is to be called 'crooked'? Is it only man who is deliberately and consciously to neglect the goal which has been fixed for his endeavours here below and swerve from the path which alone leads to his goal? Is it only man who is to allow himself to be enticed from the one straight and direct path by seductive flowers at the roadside, by paths which he sees to be good for others, by mountains which he finds in his own way, by pleasures which beckon to him on other roads?

> Obedience is the rule everywhere. All know their Master. The insect, the worm, the lion, the eagle, the power which slumbers in the terrestrial globe, which flashes in the lightning, which shapes the crystal, which opens the flower-bud, which reigns in the heart-beat the life that fills the air, that roams over the earth, that swarms in the sea, that resides in the bosom of the ground, they all serve the one God; one Will dominates them; one God commands them; one Law reigns over all. And shall man alone choose for himself defiance and disobedience? Shall he alone be unwilling to see the Master and to inquire after His law?
>
> (S. R. Hirsch, *Gesammelte Schriften*, 2nd ed., 1908, 1:139 f.)

In a further moral dimension of Rosh Hashanah, the Talmud ascribes to the 1st of Tishri God 'visiting' Sarah, Rachel and Hannah to cause them to become fruitful (*Rosh Hashanah* 10b).

The Midrash elaborates: 'Why did these great mothers suffer the agony of childlessness for so long? Because the Holy One, Blessed be He, yearned to hear their prayers and supplications' (Gen. Rab. 45:4). Did He really take pleasure in hearing these virtuous women cry? No doubt what the Midrash seeks to convey is that such exceptionally inspired men like Isaac, Joseph and Samuel are born only out of the supplications of their mothers which reached their climax on Rosh Hashanah.

Another moral nuance for the choice of the harvest season as the period of judgement is to enable the verdict to be tempered by the timely performance of charitable deeds: 'The poor are given the gleanings, the forgotten sheaves, and the corners of the fields – so that, when the Holy One, Blessed be

He, comes to sit in judgement on the world, He may judge Israel not with the quality of Divine justice, but with the quality of Divine mercy. For great is the efficacy of charity that turns the quality of strictness into the quality of mercy' (R. Yehuda Rosanes, *Parashat Derachim*).

The institution of an annual season for penitence is itself a manifestation of Divine kindness towards His creatures. 'He reviews their deeds year after year on Rosh Hashanah, so that their sins may not grow too numerous, and there may be room for forgiveness and, being few, He may forgive them. For, if He were not to remember them for a long time, their sins would multiply to such an extent as to doom the world. So this revered day assures the world of survival' (R. Aron Halevi of Barcelona, *Sepher Hachinnuch*, Commandment 311).

Anniversary of Creation

Our Sages were divided as to whether the world's creation as recounted in Genesis took place at Pesach time in the spring or, as is the accepted view, in Tishri, at the beginning of the Jewish year. According to this opinion Rosh Hashanah is actually the anniversary of the Creation of Man on the Sixth Day of Creation, while the First Day corresponds to the 25th of Ellul six days earlier.

This traditional belief that Rosh Hashanah marks the anniversary of the creation of man rather than of the universe reflects the anthropocentric world-view of Judaism — with man as the centre and purpose of Creation. Indeed, man is to be a partner with God in Creation, manifesting the Divine spark or 'image' in him. The theme is further developed in the Rosh Hashanah liturgy.

One would hardly expect to find in the *Machzor* a dissertation on cosmology, on how and why the universe came into existence. This is not because the authors of the special festival prayers were indifferent or ignorant. Indeed, most of the special Rosh Hashanah prayers were composed at a time in the Middle Ages when the great Jewish thinkers flourished. The leading Jewish philosophers – from Saadiah and Maimonides to Gersonides and Hasdai Crescas – wrote extensively on the philosophical aspects of Creation. Maimonides was even prepared to accept in principle Plato's belief in the eternity of matter as quite compatible with religious faith, a view rejected only because of certain irregularities in nature, such as the variety of colours emitted by different stars. This can only be understood if the universe is governed not by uniform laws of nature but by God's free will which allows for diversity and even miracles suspending the natural law (*Guide* 2:22–24).

Nor is the *Machzor* a book of science, philosophy or mysticism. It is a vehicle of instruction, contemplation and inspiration. In such a context, the Creation story is of relevance only in its moral ramifications.

The link between Rosh Hashanah and Creation therefore again serves purely moral ends. The liturgy spells this out in very explicit terms: 'This is the day of the world's creation (lit. conception), this is the day when all the world's creatures are mustered in judgement'. This is based on the first Mishnah in the tractate *Rosh Hashanah* over a thousand years earlier: 'On Rosh Hashanah all that come into the world pass before Him like flocks of sheep, as it is said, He Who fashions the hearts of them all, Who understands all their doings' (Ps. 33:15). We are accountable only because we are created. Were we to be the product of chance rather than choice, we could not be asked whether we have fulfilled the purpose of our existence or lived up to the demands of our Creator. Creation and judgement are interdependent.

It is also beyond the scope and objective of the *Machzor* to deal with the process of Creation *versus* evolution, although once again the great medieval Jewish thinkers did relate to the question, albeit not by scientific observation, whether of fossils or of stars being formed or dying. Science itself as we now know, is discovering and then discarding various mutually-exclusive theories. At present, the 'Big Bang' theory is in vogue. This presupposes a one-time explosion out of nothing in what we would call an act of creation, with the universe constantly expanding from that single 'Bang'.

Even the emergence of man out of lower forms of life need not be disputed. What matters is that man, whatever his physical origin, is a unique creature, endowed with intellectual and moral capacities not shared by any other form of life.

EVOLUTION AND THE UNIQUENESS OF MAN

It is noteworthy that in the biblical account of creation no special day is allotted to man. He is represented as originating, so to speak, in the evening of the same day on which the land animals, the mammals, originated. This presentation implies that the act of creation which produced man did not consist in giving him his form. In fact, as far as his body is concerned, man bears such resemblance to the highest types of mammals that he might have emerged from the soil like the other animals. Does not the Midrash itself comment on the biblical verse 'Let the earth bring forth a living soul' (Gen. 1:24) – this is the breath of the life of the first man?...

Granted, then, that the body of the first man was produced by normal generation from a species of non-human ancestors, the Divine breath that animated the body brought into existence something new which now for the first time entered into the sum of existing reality. Here was a being which could think and will and have dominion. Here was a being new, not in degree, but in kind, transcending in inner perfection all other existing beings. It was the first subsisting intelligence, and its novelty could come only from the original source when the Universe had come – from God.

(Isidore Epstein, *The Faith of Judaism*, pp. 208–11)

The Jewish Idea of Prayer

The traditional Jewish concept of prayer embraces three distinct and essential characteristics: the text is fixed, as are the times for prayer; the compositions encompass teachings as well as petitions; and the liturgy (usually worded in the plural form) is intended for congregational rather than private recitation. These three essential characteristics provide the answer to the obvious problems raised by prayer: What purpose can be served by formulating our pleas to God? Does the all-knowing God who knows our needs better than we do require their articulation of what we feel in our hearts? Still more difficult theologically, how can we hope by prayer to change His will? Our very belief in the efficacy of our petitions would seem to challenge God's immutability, and even question His justice, since we should assume that whatever fate He decrees for man is essentially just; why, and how, therefore, do we seek to reverse it?

But such questions are based on a false, indeed pagan, understanding of prayer as a means of pacifying and propitiating the deity and thus of earning its favours. It was against these perverse notions that the Hebrew Prophets directed their denunciations so fiercely when they fulminated against the heathen form of sacrifices, the original form of worship later replaced by prayer.

The Torah idea of sacrifice, *korban*, is meant to bring man near (from *karav*) to God. 'Why (offer) *unto Me* the multitude of your sacrifices; I am sated with the burnt-offerings of rams and the fat of animals' (Is. 1:11). God does not need our offerings; we need them. Prayer, if offered for the wrong motives, is likewise unacceptable: 'And when you spread out your hands I will close my eyes from you, even when you multiply prayer I will not listen…' (13).

Like sacrifices, prayer is intended to change man, not God. Its purpose is to cultivate a contrite heart, to promote feelings of humility and inadequacy, whilst encouraging reliance on Divine assistance. Through prayer, the worshipper becomes chastened, gains moral strength and intensifies the quest for spirituality, thereby turning himself into a person worthy of a response to his pleas.

SELF-IMPROVEMENT THROUGH PRAYER

> If God has decreed the good fate for a man, He requires no prayer; and if there is no such decree, how can prayer help to change the will of God in favour of a good decree? And similarly in reverse. The answer is that the main purpose of prayer is not to change the will of the Holy One Blessed Be He, Heaven forfend. But through the prayer the worshipper himself becomes changes, for he rises to a more elevated and lofty level. And just as 'a proselyte who becomes Jewish is like a new-born child,' so does the Jew when he rises from step to step represents a new person. If the decree was issued on a certain person, then through prayer which

> crushes his heart he becomes someone else, who is no longer meant by the decree.
>
> (Joseph Albo, *Sepher Ha'Ikkarim* 1425)

The Hebrew for 'pray', unlike the English, is not synonymous with 'beg' or 'petition'. *Tephilah* derives from *hitpalel*, literally 'judge oneself'; one assesses one's own insignificance and one's impotence in relation to God's omnipotence. The reflexive form indicates that prayer is directed at oneself rather than at God. In short, Jewish prayer is intended to *impress* more than to *express* oneself. The harder I pray, the more convinced I become that only God can help me, and that I need His help. Prayer thereby turns me into a better and more deserving human being; in respect of all the favours for which I ask, I realize more and more my dependence on God and my own helplessness.

That is why in our tradition prayer is fixed. The virtues to be taught are changeless. The routine instruction provided by prayer is as vital and constant for spiritual health as daily bread is for physical sustenance.

Since prayer is primarily not a channel for emotional self-expression – of baring one's heart – but an instrument for the evocation of fundamental truths that are to stir our hearts, the impact of prayer is increased when the atmosphere in which it is offered is charged with the maximum solemnity and fervour. To this end, the corporate outpourings of a congregation are clearly more impressive than the private devotions of a lone worshipper. Hence the emphasis on public prayer. And hence also the profusion of teachings and declarations in the statutory liturgy, rather than mere petitions. The ultimate aim is primarily to ennoble the petitioner by making his dependence on God ever more manifest, with a correspondingly heightened realization of his own frailty.

The Atmosphere of Prayer

<u>HOW CAN GOD 'DWELL' IN SYNAGOGUES?</u>

When King Solomon consecrated the Temple he had built – the first permanent House of Divine Worship ever erected on earth – he uttered a superb prayer in which he alluded to one of the most perplexing religious problems: 'But will God in very truth dwell on the earth? Behold, heaven and the heaven of heavens cannot contain You; how much less this house that I have built!' (I Kings 8:27).

We believe God is everywhere; infinite and omnipresent. How, then, can He be found and worshipped in 'synagogues' rather than anywhere else? Are we not just as near to Him in our homes, in the streets and fields, in the inner space of our hearts and the outer space of the universe beyond? Why, then, do we have to build Him temples and invest them with special sanctity? In what way are we closer to Him there than elsewhere?

The advances of science have given us many insights denied to former generations. Perhaps this problem, too, can be more easily understood and solved in the light of our present-day knowledge. The world is filled with a multitude of sounds carried on radio bands of different wave-lengths to every part of the universe. Thousands of radio stations constantly emit programmes of speech and song. And yet, despite the multitude of sounds surrounding us at all times, we hear none of them unless we tune in to a particular transmission on our radio receivers.

The human senses have only an extremely limited range of perception. Our ear, for instance, can hear only a tiny fraction of the sound waves (and none of the radio waves) in the air and make them audible to us. For a much larger range we need instruments, called radio sets, which transform ultrasound or electric waves so that we can hear them as sounds.

Spiritually we are constructed with similar limitations. Our human senses, made of flesh and blood, cannot perceive God, though He is everywhere around us. To transmit His Presence to us, to make us conscious of His infinite Being, we require special instruments, receiving sets called *synagogues*, through which the purely spiritual can register an impact on us.

A true house of worship has the capacity to make us sense Godliness, to enable us to hear His word, to cause us to experience His comfort. God *is* everywhere; but only in houses of God is He *felt* to be both receptive to our prayers and offering His blessings. Only there is His existence sufficiently amplified to enable us to realize that He dwells in our midst.

A radio set is a delicate apparatus, and it has to fulfil many technical requirements if it is to translate radio waves into audible sounds. A synagogue is a far more complex instrument. It seeks to transmute the intangible into something tangible; to make finite beings perceive the Infinite; to convert that which emanates from the Divine into terms sensible to humans.

To perform this unique function, a synagogue must satisfy many conditions, all designed to convey the Presence of God as a manifest reality. Inside it the worshipper is to find himself in an altogether different world, measured and constructed in purely spiritual dimensions. Its architecture, its seating arrangements, its melodies, its language, its decorum – in short, everything which makes up the totality of the worshippers experience – must be distinct from the world outside. By means of these external tokens, those who enter a synagogue and participate in its services are to feel differently, think differently, talk differently and behave differently from the way they do anywhere else.

(Immanuel Jakobovits, *The Atmosphere of Prayer*, New York, 1962)

Devotion at Prayer

Detractors of rabbinic Judaism often decry its alleged legalism which stresses the letter of the law more than its spirit, and is unduly concerned with the mechanical performance of religious duties. Nothing refutes this canard more conclusively than the laws insisting on the proper devotion while praying. Devotion (*kavanah*) means both some comprehension of the meaning of the prayers one recites, and concentrating the mind while praying.

Genuinely Jewish prayer is a feast of spirituality. It is the antithesis of the cold formality of religious services favoured by some denominations which turn acts of worship, for officiants and worshippers alike, into performances rather than outpourings of the heart and most profoundly stirring experiences, ideally to be turned into daily, or at least weekly, events.

But even among the more pious regulars, prayers no longer have the electrifying grip of former generations. The knowledge of the Siddur and the *Machzor* has become ever more deficient just when familiarity with other rabbinic texts has expanded and intensified.

MODERN MAN'S LOST ART OF PRAYER

> Modern man has lost the capacity to pray. Rare indeed are the individuals who can free their souls from the paralysing apathy of our days…from the disastrous spell of rationalism and materialistic thoughts, to pray with deep devotion for the realisation of the ultimate purpose in life. The worshipper is conscious neither of the comforting and purifying power of prayer nor of its elevating and ennobling effects, for prayer fell victim to a culture estranged from God and became degraded to an act of mere habit.
>
> (Elie Munk, *The World of Prayer*, 1954)

All religious duties should be performed with due devotion and mental concentration. Nevertheless, at least according to some opinions, the absence of such devotion does not invalidate the act except in the case of prayer, where all authorities agree that some degree of concentration is required. Thus, particularly at the openings of the *Shema* and the *Amidah*, if these were recited without proper attention, they must be repeated. For, as the great Jewish moralist, Bachya ibn Pekudah of the eleventh century put it, 'Prayer without the heart is like a body without the spirit' (*Chovot HaLevavot*). This essential condition for the validity of prayer, or at least of some of them, is also included in all later codes of Jewish law (e.g. *Shulchan Aruch, Orach Chayim*, 61 and 101).

The importance of understanding one's prayers is such that worshippers ignorant of Hebrew may pray in the vernacular (*Sotah* 7:1). But Hebrew is still the preferred medium, and the answer to not knowing it is to learn it.

Also important for the effectiveness of prayer is the frame of mind out of which it is said. The Talmud urges that 'one should never rise to pray in a mood of dejection, or indolence, or laughter, chatter, frivolity or idle talk, but only in a mood of joyful piety' (*Berachot* 31a).

A particularly striking illustration of Judaism's insistence that the ideal prayer comes not out of despondency or anguish but only out of exhilaration lies in the biblical rule that anyone defiled by contact with the dead (presumably a mourner for a close relative in the first place) cannot be admitted to the Temple until the sagging spirit is lifted through a process of purification (Num. 19:13). Synagogues are not a repair shop for broken hearts and depressed spirits. Such repairs should be carried out before entering the synagogue.

The idea that the supreme form of prayer is synonymous with jubilation is also expressed at King Solomon's consecration of the Temple – the first permanent House of God ever built on earth – when he pleaded that God may hearken, above all else, 'to the singing and to the prayer' to be uttered there (I Kings 8:28).

Some of our synagogues might be rather empty if they were out of bounds to mourners. But the finest form of worship still enjoins: 'Serve the Lord with gladness; enter His presence with singing' (Ps. 100:2).

Prayer requires constant effort and exercise. One who uses his legs only three times a year will find that he cannot walk properly even then, for his muscles will waste for lack of exercise. Similarly, he who prays only on Rosh Hashanah and Yom Kippur may find his prayers limping even on these days.

Our Sages spoke of prayer as 'A service, or labour, of the heart'. Prayer means hard work and heart work: and a heart operation is a most delicate operation.

OPERATING ON THE HEART

> Imagine a heart-surgeon bending over his patient doing a cardiac operation and thinking not of his work but of the fees due to him. So is the worshipper who, while attending a Divine service, puts his mind on business matters instead of on his prayers. As a famous 17th-century Polish preacher expressed it: 'Is this a service of the heart, when the body is in the synagogue and the mind in the market?' (Maggid of Koznitz)
>
> (Immanuel Jakobovits, *Journal of a Rabbi*, 1966)

For enhancing the fervour of our prayers, the Jewish tradition recommends both silence and crying out aloud in different contexts. This is based on what appear to be two contradictory biblical passages. The Talmud hails the example of Hannah when she pleaded for the gift of a child: 'Only her lips moved, but her voice could not be heard' (I Sam. 1:13) – which teaches that he who prays should pronounce the words with his lips without the voice being heard (*Berachot* 31a). By contrast, the citizens of Nineveh were told to 'cry mightily unto God' to avert their doom (Jonah 3:8) – implying that the voice should be raised in prayer (Ramban, end *Bo*).

Clearly, both practices apply, each according to circumstances. In general, Hannah's model should be followed, with prayers rendered in silence, though audible to one's own ears. Loud prayers should be avoided. Apart from disturbing other worshippers (*Tur Shulchan Aruch*, 111), such conduct suggests little faith, as if God could not hear silent prayer. It is also reminiscent of the false Prophets of Baal who cried out aloud when their sacrifice was spurned (I Kings 18:28; see *Berachot* 24b and Rashi) Another interesting reason for objecting to saying prayers aloud is 'so as not to put sinners to shame' [by others hearing their confessions], just as the Torah (Lev. 6:18) insists that sin-offerings and voluntary sacrifices be offered in the same place so that sinners would not be recognized (*Sotah* 32b).

But there are exceptions. They are made for those who cannot otherwise concentrate on their prayers. On Rosh Hashanah and Yom Kippur the practice is widespread, though not universally endorsed, to recite all prayers in a slightly raised voice (*Orach Chayim*, 11:3). Distracting the congregation need not then be feared, since all nowadays have Siddurim and *Machzorim* (*Mishnah Berurah*, 11).

On the other hand, the precedent in the Book of Jonah for loud utterances is intended for non-statutory compositions, such as the penitential and other poetic passages as well as songs of praise and rejoicing (*Aruch Hashulchan*, 111:8).

TEN WAYS OF ENHANCING KAVANAH

The *Sepher Derech Chayim* (*Venice*, 1618) page 67, lists ten items to enhance devotion at prayer:

1. *Torah*. Constant pursuit of Torah studies alone can engender the sincere intimacy with God which is conducive to praying with devotion and conviction.

2. *Novelty*. While the text remains fixed, every recitation of our prayers should have a freshness both of nuance and interpretation; otherwise it

becomes routine and perfunctory. [In the same spirit, the Talmud teaches that studying a passage 100 times cannot be compared to studying it 101 times (*Chagigah* 9b) – each time one discovers some novel meaning.]

3. *Need.* Moments of great need, of crisis or danger, evoke the most ardent prayers.

4. *Language.* Pray in the language that is most familiar and meaningful. You should therefore practice speaking Hebrew with your friends so that it will become natural to you.

5. *Movement.* To sway the body during prayer distracts attention, whereas standing still increases it. The habit of swaying the body, founded on the verse: 'All my bones shall say it' (Ps. 35:10), refers only to Songs of Praise, the Blessings of the *Shema* and Torah study, but not to the *Amidah*. Experience proves that standing still enhances attention, just as a person would not plead before a mortal king whilst his body shakes like the trees in the forest before the wind.

6. *Voice.* Pray in soft tones to promote attention. Loudness distracts it. True, for those who cannot concentrate, a raised voice may help to preserve the awareness of praying, but it will not advance the attention to the meaning of the prayers.

7. *Preparation.* Before commencing the service, condition your mind by silent meditation – simply sitting still for a while, removing all mundane thoughts, and thinking of the greatness of the Creator and His wonders. In earlier times, the

pious would spend an hour on such spiritual preparation before starting the service. (*Berachot*, 5:1).

8. *Entrance*. Do not proceed into the synagogue while the congregation recites the principal prayers

   so as not to interfere with the worshippers' concentration. Even in individual worship, be careful not to stand in a place where one is likely to be disturbed by passers-by.

9. *Neighbour*. Always try and render your prayers sitting near a pious person whose own devout manner of worship encourages emulation. By the same token, avoid a sinful neighbour since his presence may ensnare you to thoughts incompatible with the Divine presence.

10. *Time*. Set aside sufficient time to allow for prayers to be recited with due deliberation. A rushed service is bound to compromise the attention given to the meaning of your prayers. Sometimes it is difficult to keep pace with the speed of a public service and a slower tempo on your own may be preferable.

(Quoted in the *Siddur HaGRA* (the 'Gaon of Vilna'), Introduction from the *Sepher SHeLAH*, Amsterdam, 1598, p.250 b.)

Praying with a Congregation

The importance of congregational prayer cannot be overstressed. In fact, virtually all standard texts are composed in the plural, and are meant primarily for public recitation. Even when recited privately or silently, they are meant to identify the individual worshipper with the community, and by extension with the entire House of Israel. Likewise, the most sacred parts of the service, such as *Kaddish*, *Kedusha* and the Reading of the Torah require a *minyan* of ten adult Jews making up a minimal 'congregation'. Otherwise these parts of the service must be altogether omitted.

Public prayer is different in essence and not just in degree from private prayer at several quite unrelated levels. It is not merely an amplification of individual petitions or recitations, thereby enhancing their effectiveness.

1. Seeking blessings by prayer can be a purely selfish act. By merging one's wants with the congregation, public prayer eliminates this demerit (Moses Hasid, *Iggeret HaMussar*, 1717). This indeed is the characteristic difference between material and spiritual bounties. As the great chassidic teacher, R. Mendel of Kotsk (1788–1859) put it: 'You [in the plural] shall serve the Lord...and He will bless *your* [in the singular] bread (Ex. 23:25) – one eats *alone*, by oneself (singular), but should pray (plural) in communion with all Israel, even *when alone*'. The greatest Jewish poet and philosopher expressed a similar idea thus: 'Praying only for oneself is like...refusing to assist fellow-citizens in the repair of their walls...In a congregation, one compensates for the defects of the other' (Yehuda Halevi, 1135, *Kuzari*, 3:19).

2. To pray for others is itself the highest form of neighbourly love. In a striking rule, the summary law code, *Kitzur Shulchan Aruch* (12:2), urges that before praying one should formally accept the commandment to 'Love your neighbour as yourself', and a special formula to that effect appears in several Siddur editions. Nothing demonstrates caring for others more than praying for them. Indeed, the Talmud (*Bava Kamma* 92a) declares without qualification:

Whoever solicits mercy for the ailment of another with which he too is afflicted, his needs will be answered first, as evidenced by Abraham who prayed for the healing of Avimelech's childlessness (Gen. 20:17) was himself blessed and Sarah, his wife, bore him a child (21:1).

3. Each person is accountable both for his private deeds as an individual and also as a member of the society in which he lives. However, the individual and the community are subject to separate judgements. The *Shema* expresses this quite explicitly by using the plural in the passage dealing with reward and punishment (Deut. 11 :13 and; see Rashi) and by limiting the illustrations to forms of retribution, such as promise of rain and plentiful harvests, and the warning of drought and exile rather than individual predicaments.

On Rosh Hashanah and Yom Kippur, this distinction between the status of the individual and that of the congregation is amplified in respect of all three aspects of the synagogue service:

i. The congregation may rely more fully on the Reader's public recitation. Altogether, at this season, extra care should be taken to choose a reader with the highest religious and moral virtues, imposing in appearance and preferably married and blessed with children, 'who can spontaneously pour out his heart and plead from the depth of his soul' (*Kitzur Shulchan Aruch*, 128:7);

ii. The essential blasts of the Shofar are repeated, first before *Musaph* (originally while seated – *teki'ot d'me'yushav*) for individual worshippers, and then again during the *Amidah* or its repetition (while standing – *d'me'umad*) for the congregation (see Maimonides, *Hil. Shofar*, 3:7);

iii. Similarly, the confession of sins, a biblical commandment unique to Yom Kippur, is recited privately at the end of the silent *Amidah*, and then in the middle of the public repetition by the reader collectively with the congregation.

SWAYING DURING STUDY AND PRAYER

> They used to have only one text (manuscript) for many readers and students, and they were unable to look in together but only one after another. They therefore had to lean their head and read, before turning back again, to let the second and the third do likewise, the book lying on the ground. This resulted in a continual bending and sitting up. And it became a habit...
>
> (Yehuda Halevi, *Kuzari*, 1135, 2:80)

Another explanation:

> And when the people saw it (the Revelation at Sinai), they trembled' (Ex. 20:15) – therefore people sway during the study of Torah which was given in awe and trembling.
>
> (*Baal Haturim*, on Ex. 20:15)

THE VIRTUE OF CONGREGATIONAL PRAYER

> Congregational Prayer is heard at all times; even if sinners were present, the Holy One, Blessed be He, does not reject the prayer of the many. Therefore, a person should attach himself to the congregation and not pray on his own, so long as he is able to join a congregation...For prayer is not heard at any time except in the house of prayer, and whoever has a synagogue in his town and does not worship therein deserves to be called a bad neighbour.
>
> (Maimonides, *Mishneh Torah, Hil. Tephila,* 8:1)

The Rosh Hashanah and Yom Kippur Texts and Commentaries

The special basic texts for Rosh Hashanah and Yom Kippur are actually very short indeed. Maimonides in his great Code (end of *Sepher Ahavah*) features the entire service, including the insertions or changes in the usual formulations, in less than two pages. That is the extent of the statutory High Holyday liturgy, for both private and public recitation.

The rest are embellishments, made up mainly of religious poetry from various periods and locations in the Middle Ages. Stirring and magnificent as many of them are, in the structure of the liturgy they are still of relatively secondary significance compared to the essential texts of the *Shema* and the *Amidah* around which the entire morning service is constructed. Thus, the *Amidah* is far more central and fundamental than, for instance, the *Unetaneh Tokeph* (in the *Musaph*) or even the *Aleinu* prayer attributed to Joshua.

The later liturgical compositions are known as *Piyutim*, and their authors as *Paytanim*, from the Greek and Latin words for *poet*. Some of these were originally spontaneous compositions by gifted *chazanim* which soon became popular, much as in later generations cantorial renderings in common usage in our synagogues. The form of some such poetry also gradually became standardized. For instance, a poem with a repetitive refrain was known as a *pizmon* (again from the Greek and Latin *psalmos*, with the letter 'l' dropped, as in English 'Psalm' where the 'l' is not pronounced).

According to Leopold Zunz, the pioneering nineteenth-century German-Jewish scholar of the *Juedische Wissenschaft*, there were some 1500 liturgical poets, of whom he names 500 – most of them living in Muslim Spain. Over a thousand compositions are known of four authors alone. Authors include the greatest poets like Solomon Ibn Gabirol and Yehuda Halevi as well as leading talmudists like Rashi and Rabbenu Gershom, who in the eleventh century proclaimed the famous edict against polygamy.

The most famous and most prolific liturgical poet was Eleazar Kallir, variously placed between the tenth and seventh centuries, or even much earlier in the talmudic period. He left over two hundred compositions, many of them incorporated into our regular Festival liturgy. Both the Franco-German (Ashkenazi) and the Spanish-Provençal (Sephardi) communities produced outstanding *Paytanim*; the former concentrating more on God–Israel relations along national lines, while the latter laid the stress on man–Creator bonds with universalist overtones (Rapaport 1838, p. 184). From all of them 'we hear not only the echo of these poets' hearts, but the pulse in the veins of the nation; we feel the warmth of its soul, and we sense its aspirations and its feelings, its woes and its pains' (Chief Rabbi J. L. Landau of Johannesburg, in *Otzar Yisrael*, 8:222).

But the acclaim or even sanction for the insertion of these pieces of literary art in the regular liturgy was by no means unanimous. The leading opponent was Abraham Ibn Ezra (in his commentary on *Kohelet*, 5:1), notwithstanding his own legacy of some 150 *Piyutim*, including a magnificent contribution to the table songs for Shabbat still widely popular in many Jewish homes.

Ibn Ezra's opposition is founded on four reasons: (1) The *Piyutim* are often written in 'riddles and parables', which can hardly be understood by the worshipper; (2) the Hebrew grammar is deficient, and the language altogether a mix between Hebrew and Aramaic, biblical and talmudic; (3) the language used itself has major flaws; and (4) the text relies on *Midrashim* and *Aggadot* instead of on the plain meaning of the relevant passages.

Other opponents objected to the interruptions in the statutory prayers (so notably the Gaon of Vilna among many other leading authorities). Additional objections concerned the inclusion of reliance on angels and intermediaries in pleading before God, as well as the burden placed upon the community by drawing out the services. Thus the thirteenth-century Spanish poet R. Yehuda Al-Harizi complains that 'the Chazan would drag out the *Piyutim* until midday, an hour when the people would be asleep or have left the synagogue' (*Tachkemoni*, 24). It was even argued that Kallir composed his *Piyutim* only for his own generation and not for later times (*P'ri Chadash*, 113).

But many leading authorities in the Middle Ages at least tolerated these additions (and interruptions) in the Festival Services, if only out of respect for their saintly authors and out of concern not to alter widely established customs (R. Abraham ibn Daud; Rabbenu Tam; MaHaRIL; and especially R. Moshe Isserles, *Orach Chayim*, 619:1 gloss).

The most celebrated defence of *Piyutim* is found in a lengthy Responsum by R. Elazar Fleckeles of Prague written in 1793 (*Teshuvah Me'Ahavah*, 1:1). The polemic is so magnificent in style and scholarly in content that it is reproduced in some *Machzorim*, such as the popular *Korban Aharon* (*Mattei Levi*, Berditchev, 1818).

Fleckeles first disputes Ibn Ezra's allegations and challenges – above all his criticism of Kallir whose work was hailed by the most eminent scholars over the ages. Fleckeles addresses his Responsum to 'my beloved disciple' and pleads with him: 'You should know that I am angry not with the scoffer but with him who praises the scoffer. For whoever has eyes to see and ears to hear will recognize and understand in his heart that all the words of Kallir are full of the splendour of wisdom, radiating the light of insight, and with the spirit of his mouth illuminating obscure aggadic and midrashic passages...' He then provides in superlative terms a long list of outstanding rabbinical leaders describing the majesty of liturgical poetry as a most profound religious experience inspiring the loftiest thoughts. This is followed by a detailed listing of particularly instructive *Piyutim* enhanced by many laudatory classic sources.

By contrast, Fleckeles berates a latter generation of liturgical poets, some 150 years later, because their works lack grace and wisdom. They rely unduly on the intercession of angels, as in the compositions which appear in between the 30 statutory shofar sounds on Rosh Hashanah.

A Short Survey of Machzor Commentaries and English Translations

The *Machzor* as we know it is in its main features less than one thousand years old. Although Philo of Alexandria nearly two thousand years ago mentions all-day Yom Kippur services (see I. Ellbogen, *Der Juedische Gottesdienst*, 1924, p. 149), Leopold Zunz (*Ritus der Juden*, 1919, p. 95) argues from a late talmudic passage (*Chullin* 101b) that early in the fourth century synagogue services on Yom Kippur were of the same duration as those on ordinary Sabbaths. In any event, the texts in our present *Machzor*, for the most part, were composed much later.

Equally striking is the fact that commentaries on the *Piyutim* are about as old as these liturgical compositions themselves. Zunz (*Ritus*, 22ff.; 194ff.) lists the names of 70 *Machzor* commentators, some from as early as the eleventh century.

The total output of liturgical poetry was quite enormous. Philip Birnbaum (in his Introduction to the *High Holydays Prayer Book*, 1951) estimates that there were altogether 35,200 metrical compositions which were inspired by the synagogue services, and Israel Davidson (*Thesaurus of Medieval Hebrew Poetry*) counts 2,485 liturgical poets who contributed to this extensive literature.

A major turning-point occurred with Gutenberg's invention of printing in 1436. This event, which had a powerful impact on Jewish literature generally, began to eliminate the primacy of, and dependence on, the previously indispensable rendering of *Chazanim* for following the service (see Zunz, *Ritus*, 145). As the printed *Machzor* thus gradually moved to centre-stage in the service, a focus of complaint arose against inordinate spending on clothes and not enough on beautiful *Machzorim* (Chaim Palache, Izmir, 1788–1869, quoted by Agnon, *Days of Awe*, p. 57).

The earliest scholarly authority on the *Machzor* was Wolf Heidenheim (Germany, 1757–1832). His nine-volume *Machzor* (Roedelheim, 1800–02), rated as the greatest work on our liturgy (Goldschmidt, *Rosh Hashanah Machzor*, p. 59), included the first German translation (in Hebrew characters), a Hebrew commentary, and an introduction on the *Machzor*'s literary history.

The next monumental Hebrew commentary was the widely popular *Korban Aharon* by Aaron, son of Jehiel Michael of Michailishki (Vilna region) first published in 1818. Based partly on earlier manuscript commentaries, this valuable work consists of three parts: *Mattei Levi*, explaining the meaning of the passage; *Beth Levi*, interpreting the words used and their sources; and *Ma'aseh Ereg*, discoursing at greater length on talmudic and midrashic allusions on themes suggested by the text.

Finally, there is the comprehensive critical edition by Daniel Goldschmidt (Jerusalem, 1970). This features not only the liturgical texts of various rites, some drawn from early printed and manuscript versions, including textual variations, but also a comprehensive scholarly commentary, often discovering sources not otherwise found. Particularly valuable in this edition are the comprehensive introductions which range over the entire gamut of authorship, style, history and components of the Festival services.

Rites, Translations and English Editions

Whatever religious, political, cultural, regional and ancestral traits have fragmented the Jewish people almost throughout its history, certain features of our common heritage have never been displaced or disputed for any length of time. These have preserved our essential unity and continuity. For the mainstream of the Jewish people, there has always been only one Torah, one *Tenach*, one text of the Talmudim, one broadly-agreed version of Rashi, Rambam, and the *Shulchan Aruch*. Another unifying factor has been the Hebrew language as the holy tongue of all sections of our people.

True, the Mishnah (*Sotah*, 7:1) rules that both the *Shema* and the Statutory Prayer can be recited in any language one understands, because – as the Talmud (33a) comments – 'Prayer seeks compassion' and must therefore come from the heart in familiar accents.

But this applies only to personal or special prayers. All later authorities to the present day insist that the traditional fixed prayer handed down from the Men of the Great Synagogue over two thousand years ago must be recited in Hebrew, and any departure from this tradition is to be deprecated as an evil breach of Jewish solidarity over the ages, an affront to Jewish unity which has led to similarly expunging references to Zion and Jerusalem from our prayers (*Mishnah Berurah*, 101:13; *Aruch Hashulchan, Orach Chayyim* 101:9 and 102:4).

The only major exception to the rule of virtual uniformity throughout the House of Israel all over the world is the poetry of the synagogue service. We have already noted the fierce debate on whether to recite such insertions in the Statutory Prayers altogether. But even where the practice was widely accepted, as it was in most communities whatever their rites, the actual texts varied widely from locality to locality, often to the point of losing all identical traces. The distinctions were not only by the usual broad geographical divisions, such as between Ashkenazim and Sephardim, or the Rumanian, Italian, German, Polish, North African and Yemenite versions which often had very little, sometimes nothing, in common with each other. There were even traditional versions limited to single communities only.

A very brief summary of the most significant dates and places in the evolution of this remarkable literature will testify to its wealth and diversity.

The first *Machzor* ever printed, of the Roman rite, appeared in Soncino in 1485, and was thus among the earliest incunabula. In the succeeding centuries, virtually all European and North African communities produced their own *Machzor* versions, each with its own poetic texts. Noteworthy examples are the Rumanian rite (Venice and Constantinople, 1602), the Sephardi rite (Salonika, 1694), the German rite (Augsburg, 1636), the German and Polish rite (Venice, 1654), and the rite of R. Isaac Luria (ARI) from which developed later several chassidic versions (Constantinople, 1768). The North African communities also produced their own versions, such as Algiers (1740) and Tunis (Pisa, 1794). Often local rites were limited to single communities, such as the Provençal papal states of Avignon, Carpentras and Montpelier which each had their own *Machzor*, as did Frankfurt (1625), Worms (in manuscript), and Tripoli (Venice, 1648).

The first translated *Machzor*, into Italian in Hebrew script, appeared in Bologna as early as 1538. But it was not until 1787 that the first English translation, by A. Alexander and Abraham Frankel, was published in London. Soon thereafter (London, 1794), a more widely accepted translation by David Levi began to serve the English-speaking world, until it was rivalled by David Aaron di Sola's translation (London, 1860), to be replaced almost 50 years later by the Routledge edition.

There are now three popular English editions of the *Machzor*, each serving an entirely different purpose. For long by far the most widely used in Anglo-Jewish homes and synagogues is the *Service of the Synagogue, A New Edition of the Festival Prayers with an English Translation in Prose and in Verse*, based on Wolff Heidenheim's work, and edited by Jacob Davis and Naftali Adler, first published by Routledge and Kegan Paul Ltd, London, 1906. It is generally known as the Routledge *Machzor*. While the text is accurate and authentic according to the Polish rite as generally accepted in Britain and the Commonwealth countries, the presentation is unimaginative, set in monotone type and left without any commentary or notes, other than a list of the liturgical authors. The translation is scholarly and similar in style to the rendering used by the Reverend Simeon Singer in his *Authorised Daily Prayer Book*, including the archaisms so much in vogue at the turn of the century. The translation of some of the liturgical poetry appears in often very beautiful poetic renderings, notably those by Israel Zangwill and Nina Salamon.

Much more elaborate and more modern is the *High Holyday Prayer Book* by Philip Birnbaum, first published in 1951 in New York. The translation has a more contemporary ring, and the concise annotations provide essential details on the origins, meaning and authorship of the texts. Historically very useful is the Introduction, to which we have already referred.

The latest and now most popular edition belongs to the ArtScroll series, probably the largest Jewish publishing venture in history. Both the translation and the commentary are quite distinctive, intended for a fast-growing new market of yeshiva or girls' seminary-trained readers who insist above all on traditional authenticity. From the striking binding to the beautiful graphics, the extremely attractive production adorns an attitude of mind characterized by the single word 'anthologized' used for the commentary, because no statement is original but must be based on 'approved' sources.

This new edition, which provides introductory notes and self-contained essays on a wide range of subjects related to the text and yet presents some basic Jewish concepts, seeks to introduce the worshipper to the spirit of the High Holydays as much as to the prayers distinguishing them. It aims at helping to use the holiest moments of our lives for a deeper appreciation of Jewish values and virtues, turning the renewal of each year into the renewal of the Jewish spirit through the incomparable stimulants evoked by our prayers to the mind and to the heart alike.

Some Machzor Themes

- *Adon Olam* – The Creator's Transcendence and Immanence: introducing daily prayer by addressing Him as 'Master' and as 'My God'.

- *Yigdal* – Unique position of Maimonides by providing the liturgy's only philosophical composition, although his definition of Thirteen Articles of Faith was at first fiercely disputed: the fundamentals of Jewish belief.

- *Netilat Yadayim* and *Asher Yotzar* – Cleanliness and health: first daily blessing for the gift of health and its wonders in self-repair and expulsion of wastes. Blessings as a reminder of Divine gifts.

- *Birkat Hatorah* – Spiritual Health: public Torah readings have a beginning and end, therefore opening and closing blessings; whereas Torah learning is encumbent without limit 'by day and by night' and therefore only one daily opening blessing; the supreme importance of study in Judaism.

- *Baruch She'amar* – Parallel to the ten *Ma'amarot* of Creation.

- *Shirat Hayam* – The role and importance of song in prayer and study. The musical mode or motif (*nusach*) for the High Holyday services are clearly distinct from the rest of the year. There are three main modes that are used for the Evening (*ma'ariv*), Morning (*Shacharit*) and Additional (*Musaph*) Services on Rosh Hashanah and Yom Kippur, which also includes the *Neilah* 'concluding' service. The officiant conducting the service must be familiar with these modes in order to create the atmosphere of the occasion.

- *Misod Hachamim* – Reader's personal prayers: the role of *Shaliach Tzibbur* in public worship.

- *Avinu Malkenu* – Structure based on weekday *Amidah*. Father/King relationship.

- *Lema'an Harugim al Shem Kodshecha* – Martyrdom in Jewish thought, law and history.

- *The Thirteen Divine Attributes* – Positive and Negative (Maimonides).

- *Readings of the Law* – Avoidance of both obvious themes: Creation story, and teachings on judgements (extensive passages on rewards and punishments). Instead, story of emergence of moral law with Abraham and its continuity with birth of first Jewish child. Three Jewish mother prototypes: Sarah, Rachel and Hannah. The role of the woman in Judaism.

- *The Akedah* – The religious response to the Holocaust: Jewish martyrdom through the ages. The problem of Theodicy.

- Rachel as the eternal comforter of Israel and guarantor of the Return to Zion – Why Rachel?

- *The Shofar* – its meaning: beginning of Jewish history, Revelation at Sinai, Rosh Hashanah and Redemption. Oldest musical instrument, yet drawing more Jews than any concert, protest or demonstration. The significance of different sounds.

- *Musaph Amidah* – Unique construction.

- *Aleinu* – Particularism and universalism in Judaism.

- *Malchuyot* – Three cardinal principles: Existence of God, Retribution and Revelation. Parallel to three sections of *Shema*.

- *Birkat Kohanim* – Blessing out of love. Blessing the nations as a 'Kingdom of Priests': the Jewish purpose.

- *Eyn Keloheinu* – Answers and questions: the sequence of faith, but not blind faith.

- *Second Aleinu* – The Messianic hope in Judaism.

Biblical Readings for Rosh Hashanah

Both the Torah and Haftorah readings for Rosh Hashanah are significant and unusual not only for what they contain but even more for what they do not feature. As a rule, all Festival readings deal with the major theme of the day. Pesach, Shavu'ot and Succot feature, respectively, different aspects of the Exodus from Egypt, the Revelation at Sinai with the Ten Commandments, and the passage dealing with the special precepts applicable to Succot, while the last days present the Festival cycle as a whole. On Yom Kippur, too, the readings relate to the special Temple ritual on that unique day as well as to the subjects of purity and fasting.

On Rosh Hashanah there is no such link. The two most obvious themes are missing altogether. As the traditional 'birthday of Creation' a suitable Torah reading might have been the first chapter of Genesis. Or else, as the Day of Judgment, any of the many references to reproof and repentance might have been fitting. The Prophetical books in particular are replete with stirring calls for a return to righteousness and spiritual regeneration. All this is completely ignored.

Instead, all four readings deal with the origins of our people rather than the origins of the world. There appear portraits of the founders of Judaism and the Jewish people. Highlights are presented on Abraham and Sarah, the birth and the sacrifice of Isaac, Rachel being comforted on the exile of her children, and Hannah pleading for the gift of a child who turned out to be Samuel, the founder of Israel's royal dynasty.

In the choice of these subjects lies the most profound message of Judaism. Physical creation, the making of heaven and earth, is only a means to the end of spiritual fulfilment. The world was not complete and its purpose not assured until the emergence of monotheism with its vision of social justice and the brotherhood of man through Abraham, and until continuity was assured for the birth of Isaac and the promise of eventual Redemption through David's seed. That is the true meaning of Rosh Hashanah in recalling the birth of man and his destiny.

Our Sages express this idea in a striking Midrash. When God created the world, beginning with *Beth*, the second letter of the Hebrew alphabet – *Bereshith Bara* – the first letter, *Aleph*, complained to God for having been overlooked by his junior. And God comforted the *Aleph*: Your turn will come for an even more momentous Divine act; the Ten Commandments will start with *Aleph* – *Anochi* – 'I am the Lord your God'.

What does this fanciful dialogue between a letter of the alphabet and God mean? Physical creation, the universe with all its endless powers and wonders, is only the 'B' of Creation. Its primary feature, the 'A' of calling all this into being is the moral law, the revealed will of God, which is the purpose of all existence, and without which all creation would relapse into chaos.

At another level, the same message is conveyed by a further Midrash, related to the Rosh Hashanah Torah reading, regarding the primacy in the Jewish purpose.

Twice Abraham is told *Lech Lecha* – 'Go you'. 'Go you to the land which I will show you', to what is destined to become the Land of Israel, and again 'Go you to the land of Moriah', to the place which I will show you for the sacrifice of Isaac. And we do not know, say the Sages, which of the two commands, though identically worded, is the more beloved to God. The Midrash ends: 'Since it states "Go to the land of Moriah" we know this command is the more precious.'

How so? For the earlier 'Go', two reasons are given: one to get away from 'your land, your birth-place, and your father's home', and the other in order to reach the land of your destination. Therefore, going to the land is only half the purpose of the order. Whereas the second 'Go' gives only a single reason: To get to the destination of the place of Abraham's and Isaac's supreme trial in the ultimate service of God, the site on which the Temple in Jerusalem would eventually be built. That is the sole objective of the order and not merely half of it; therefore its value is superior.

There is to the Jewish people a national purpose linked with its soil, and a universal purpose linked with its soul. A physical and a spiritual destiny. Of the two, the latter is superior. There is no purpose to living in the Land, to national fulfilment, if this is not to serve the superior objective of turning the Land itself into a beacon of light and inspiration to the entire world.

The theme is a constant in Jewish thought, and nowhere more so than in relation to Rosh Hashanah which is to give direction to the entire year, as the head guides the whole body.

Three Women Heading the New Year

On Rosh Hashanah, the Torah and Haftorah readings deal extensively with three women. Women give birth, as it were, not only to human life but to the primary message of Judaism to inspire the rest of the year.

Men and women were neither created nor intended to be identical. They each have their own unique role. In some respects Judaism gives priority to women over men in identical circumstances. For instance, they must be freed or ransomed first from captivity – for fear of abuse. Again, the magnificent ode to the 'woman of valour' in the Book of Proverbs has no parallel for the male. Such women – combining outstanding leadership roles with profound piety and scholarship – are legion throughout Jewish history. As early as in biblical times, Deborah, a *Judge*, served as head of state.

In modern times it was a learned woman who suggested that the blessing men recite every morning praising God that 'He has not made me a woman' was really a singular tribute to women. Men, she contended, have every reason to thank God that they are spared the pangs of childbirth and other periodic travails endured by women. She saw in this blessing a deep sensitivity for the extra burdens borne by the female sex – to which men should respond with caring and understanding.

The sexes differ not only physically but physiologically, emotionally and therefore also in their religious needs and responses. In basic human rights and duties they are equal. Jewish criminal law, for instance, makes no distinction between them – the same imperatives, the same penalties and the same legal procedures.

But where the differences are implanted in nature to make them unequal, the law reflects this. Thus, the duty of procreation, as a religious precept, is incumbent only on men. Unlike them, women have a natural urge for parenthood. Chava (Eve) was so called because she represents 'the mother of all life (*chai*). Adam, by contrast, was not called *chayim*, for he is not correspondingly 'the father of all life'. He therefore has to make up for his deficiency in instinct or yearning by a Divine command. Torah and nature complement, not duplicate, each other.

Products of Prayer

Significantly, the biblical readings on Rosh Hashanah introduce us to three archetypal Jewish women: Sarah – mother of Isaac, the first Jewish child to be born; Rachel – personifies hope and comfort; and Hannah – mother of Samuel who anointed Israel's first kings, including David, the forebear of the Messiah.

All three suffered the long anguish of barrenness. They all prayed for a child – the greatest gift of all, and according to a tradition, their prayers were answered on Rosh Hashanah – presumably because their pleas then rose to their peak of intensity. As if to say that children like Isaac, Joseph and Samuel are not born by mere chance but are the product of total commitment to the Creator of life and the absolute submission to His will, achieved through prayer.

A look at these readings will reveal that they serve as the embodiment of the message of Rosh Hashanah.

Sarah – The More Perceptive Parent

Sarah argued with Abraham. Their son Isaac could not be raised with Hagar's son Ishmael and become a successor to Abraham. Abraham could not see it, but Sarah prevailed, and Hagar and her son were sent away.

In the next generation the experience was replicated. Isaac, when nearly blind, could not see that Esau was unfit to receive the blessing that would perpetuate Abraham's tradition. Rebecca saw it clearly, and resorted to a ruse to prove to her husband how easily he could be deceived. When the stratagem worked, Isaac confirmed the blessing to Jacob.

In the case of a child of a mixed marriage, it is the mother's faith that prevails. Her religious influence on the child is presumed to be dominant. In such conflict situations, the mother's is the more reliable claim.

Yitzchak – He shall have the Last Laugh

Another profound religious message for Rosh Hashanah is woven around the unusual name given by Divine direction even before his birth to the first Jewish child (Gen. 21:3). *Yitzchak* means 'he shall laugh'. The promise that Abraham at the age of 100 and Sarah at 90 would still be blessed with a child to preserve their heritage and bequeath it to future generations produced disbelief and laughter. 'Whoever will hear will laugh at me' (21:6), exclaimed Sarah herself. She laughed (18:11); Abraham laughed (17:17); they themselves found the idea laughable. But they were assured the promise would be fulfilled, and when born, their son shall be called *Yitzchak* (17:19) – he will have the last laugh.

His birth shall mock the mockers.

This has been the story of Jewish life throughout the ages. People ridiculed the ability of the old and devout generation to reproduce themselves by giving birth to a new youth. The old immigrant generation themselves were resigned to their disappearance, doubting that any young generation would be born to perpetuate the traditions of the past. Everybody mocked and sneered. Today they sneer or laugh no longer. A new generation of Isaacs has been born, now the one and only growth element within the Jewish people. The rest are disappearing by marrying out, opting out and through an abnormally low natural increase – contrasting with the phenomenal proliferation of the new Isaacs.

The assurance that this reborn generation will have the last laugh inspired Jewish hope and confidence at all times. The story of Yitzchak's birth has been repeated throughout Jewish history to the present-day, with more intensive Jewish learning and practice than ever before in modern times.

First Day Rosh Hashanah – The Origins of the Jewish People

The usual rule is that the Torah reading on Festivals relates to the historical event traditionally associated with that date in the Jewish Calendar. Historically, Rosh Hashanah marks the anniversary of the world's creation (at least according to one opinion recorded in the Talmud).

The Torah reading on Rosh Hashanah should therefore consist of the Creation story at the beginning of Genesis.

Yet, on Rosh Hashanah we read not about the origins of our material world, but the origins of the Jewish people – the birth of Isaac, the first Jewish child, and the Divine commandment to sacrifice him as the ultimate test of Abraham's loyalty to his Creator.

The story of Isaac's birth has a particularly poignant ring in view of the name given to him well before his birth. Abraham was told that his barren and ageing wife would be blessed with a child, and when this promise would be fulfilled, Abraham was told 'and you shall call him Yitzchak' – meaning 'and he shall laugh'.

In fact, the promise itself would produce only laughter.

The word laughter is constantly used. The idea that Abraham and Sarah, in their advanced years, would still be blessed with a child was simply laughable. 'Whoever will hear of it, will laugh at me'. Sarah herself laughed, and so did Abraham. Such a promise was the cause of much merriment. But Abraham was told, 'And you shall call his name Yitzchak' – meaning 'and *he* shall laugh'. When he is finally born he shall have the last laugh and ridicule his detractors.

That has been the story of Jewish rebirth throughout history. When Jews asserted they were an eternal people, destined in the face of all their trials and tribulations to survive and to be reborn, the world laughed. But in the end the reborn Yitzchaks shall have the last laugh, perpetuating the heritage of Abraham, when all others ridiculed such a promise and such a hope.

Second Day Rosh Hashanah – The Sacrifice of Isaac

The theme of the Torah reading on the Second Day is 'The Binding of Isaac'.

Here was at last the promised son and heir of Abraham. All the hopes of Abraham and Sarah had revolved around this child.

And no sooner did this promised child grow up to assume his destined role than the father was told to sacrifice him in a supreme test of his faith.

This trial has become the central feature of Rosh Hashanah. It explains the recourse to the Shofar, 'the ram's horn' symbolizing the animal eventually sacrificed in place of Isaac, and constantly invoked to prove Israel's loyalty over the generations.

By virtue of this sacrifice, Israel seeks forgiveness and atonement, particularly at this season of Creation, and the purpose of human life is once again to be restored and re-asserted.

The Shofar is a clarion call when the moral purpose discovered by Abraham is for the first time to be transmitted to a new generation, in the same way as Rosh Hashanah transmits his commitment to yet another new generation.

Haftorah for First Day Rosh Hashanah – Hannah's Prayer

If the Readings of the Law on Rosh Hashanah deal with the first Jewish birth and the trial of Abraham in being commanded to sacrifice his son Isaac, the Prophetic readings on both days of Rosh Hashanah deal with two principal mothers of the Jewish people, their long barrenness while waiting for the gift of a child, and the eventual fulfilment of their prayers.

On the First Day, the story relates to Hannah and her moving prayer for the blessing of a child, to be named Samuel, and eventually destined to establish the kingdom first of Saul, and later of David.

> And Hannah spoke in her heart; only her lips moved, but her voice could not be heard; therefore Eli thought she had been drunk. And Eli said unto her: 'How long will you be drunk? Put away your wine

> from you'. And Hannah answered and said: 'No my lord, I am a woman of sorrowful spirit; I have drunk neither wine nor strong drink, but I poured out my soul before the Lord'
>
> (I Sam. 1:13–15)

Several biblical personages contributed to the early history of Jewish prayer – starting with the Patriarchs, who traditionally instituted the three daily prayers and including Moses whose Song at the Red Sea features in every morning prayer. But none determined the laws on prayer more than Hannah when she poured out her heart for the gift of a child. Hers became the model on which all recitations of pleas and texts were to be based. Some of the most fundamental rules are derived from her example. Thus the Talmud, followed by the Codes, rules that in praying the worshipper should direct his heart (i.e. pray with devout attention) pronouncing the words that they are audible to himself but not to others (who should merely see the lips moving), without raising the voice, doing so in a sober state, unaffected by alcohol (*Berachot* 31a; *Orach Chayim*, 98–101).

Out of such a prayer, the Prophet Samuel was born – but not until after his mother had vowed she would consecrate her offspring to the Lord 'all the days of his life' from birth.

Thus did a woman teach scores of generations how to pray, and thus did she raise the Prophet destined to inaugurate the Messianic dynasty.

Our Sages relate a tradition whereby Hannah became pregnant and had her prayers answered on Rosh Hashanah, no doubt reflecting the belief that only when prayer reaches its most passionate climax on Rosh Hashanah can responses be assured.

Hannah's prayer became the basis for some of the standard formulations of our most passionate petitions before God, such as the plea: 'The Lord brings down to the grave, and brings up. He makes poor, and makes rich; He brings low and lifts up. He raises up the poor out of the dust, and lifts up the needy from the dunghill...For the pillars of the earth are the Lord's, and He has set the world upon them. He will guard the feet of his saints, and the wicked shall be silent in darkness; for no man shall prevail by his strength...The Lord shall judge the ends of the earth; He shall give strength unto His king, and exalt the horn of His anointed.'

Prayer is answered when it reaches the ecstasy of Rosh Hashanah, and the loftiness of the Days of Awe. That is when barrenness gives way to the supreme gift of life and continuity.

Haftorah for Second Day Rosh Hashanah – Rachel: Mother of Comfort and National Return

Like the other Matriarchs, Rachel had also for long awaited the gift of a child. Rachel became not only the mother of Jacob's two youngest children, Joseph and Benjamin, but inspired by the prophecy of Jeremiah, recited in this Haftorah, she became also the principal source of comfort for the Jewish people, the guarantor that despite their exile and tribulations, their sufferings will come to an end and they will eventually return to Zion, seeing it rebuilt. *V'shavru banim* provides a profound interpretation. She died so young on entering the holiness of the Land of Israel

> Thus says the Lord: A voice is heard on high. Bitter weeping as Rachel weeps for her children. She refuses to be comforted, for they are no more.

> Thus says the Lord: Withhold your voice from weeping and your eyes from tears. For there is a reward for your work...and there is hope for your latter end...*And your children shall return* to their border.
>
> (Jer. 31:15–17)

Why Rachel? Why not Abraham, or Isaac, or Jacob, or Sarah, or Rebecca? Why did they not weep when their children went into exile? Why were they not promised there would be an end, and the children would come back?

A striking commentary and interpretation by Nachmanides (Spain, thirteenth century) may provide the answer. The biblical laws of incest proscribe a marriage between a man and two sisters (Lev. 18:18). How then could Jacob be married to Leah and Rachel? According to Nachmanides, all laws of the Torah were given primarily for the Land of Israel, because of its superior sanctity. This applies especially to the moral laws: any violation could 'spew out' the Land's inhabitants (28). Therefore, so long as Jacob was outside the Land he could live with the two sisters. But once they entered the Holy Land, the younger (whose marriage was against the law) had to die (Ramban, Lev. 18:25).

And so Rachel laid down her young life for the sanctification of the Land. She wept when her children, on defiling the Land, were driven from it. But only she could also be reassured: There is a reward, there is hope. The children will return, and she, Mother Rachel, symbolizing the promise, will stretch out her mother's arms to receive them.

We witnessed this physically in 1967 when her tomb came under sovereign Jewish control and she was reunited with her children in scenes of indescribable jubilation.

The promise of a spiritual reunion with her children still alienated from her by the millions is yet to be fulfilled. But she, by her own life and sacrifice, guarantees it: children born to be Jews, however estranged from their faith, will return, and Rachel will greet them with her maternal embrace. They will earn their title to the Land by keeping it sacred. The title-deeds to the Land will be earned to become theirs.

The Role of Women

Of the heroes mentioned in the four Rosh Hashanah readings, three are women: Sarah, Rachel and Hannah. Theirs is evidently the key role in the origin and the destiny of the Jewish people.

This pre-eminence of women bears further scrutiny.

The Torah reading on the First Day tells the story of Sarah driving out Hagar and her son, Ishmael. Abraham protested, but was told: 'Listen to her voice'. She knew better that Isaac could not be raised as Abraham's heir living together with Ishmael. A generation later the same argument occurred between Isaac and Rebecca. Isaac wanted to give his blessing to Esau; he was blind and could not see that Esau only pretended to be a Jacob, worthy of the succession. Rebecca knew better, but she had to convince her husband that his sight was indeed defective and that Esau only pretended to be a Jacob. By a clever stratagem, she succeeded to convince her husband how easily he could be deceived, and the moment he found out, he confirmed the blessing to Jacob.

Mothers have a keener eye in discerning the qualities of their children, and they play a superior role in ensuring the continuity of the parents' blessings to their children.

Man and Woman in the Scheme of Creation

Man and woman were equally created in the image of God (Gen. 1:27).

This essential equality is also expressed in a remarkable characteristic of the Hebrew language. In the vernacular – English, French or German, for instance – entirely different words are used for male and female: Man-woman, son-daughter, brother-sister, uncle-aunt. In Hebrew, the word is the same only the gender changes: *Ish-Ishah, Ben-Bat, Ach-Achot, Dod-Dodah*. In other words, in contrast to other languages, Hebrew makes them identical, differing only in gender.

Nevertheless, equal as they are, they are not identical, and each have their distinct role. They differ in that he is active whilst she is passive; he gives and she receives. This is reflected in the marriage act.

All Mankind United

ובכן תן פחדך...
ובכן תן כבוד...
ובכן צדיקים...

These three paragraphs recited in every High Holyday *Amidah* constitute one of the most profound liturgical compositions. They succinctly survey the entire panorama of the noblest aspirations of mankind, of the Jewish people, and of righteous men.

The order is significant, moving from the general to the particular. The first precedent for this format is found in the Torah's intimation of the order for the Grace-After-Meals. According to the Talmud, each word of the biblical precept is the basis for a separate benediction: 'And You shall bless' – refers to sustaining the entire universe; 'For the Land' – refers to the gift of the Land of Israel; and 'The good' – refers to the rebuilding of Jerusalem. Thus, the World – the Land – the City. Similarly, the Seven Blessings under the Chupah start with the Creation of the universe and of man, continue with the national plea for rejoicing Zion with her children, and culminate with the joy of bride and groom, first separately and then jointly in their togetherness.

Nowhere is the universal destiny embracing all mankind encapsulated more beautifully than in the yearning 'that they may all form one single band to do Your will with a perfect heart…that Your Name be revered above all that You have created.'

When monotheism will unite all mankind in the worship of the common Creator 'as a single band', even then national and religious distinctiveness shall not be obliterated. Hence, we next seek 'glory for Your people…joy for Your Land, and gladness for Your city,' longing for the 'clear shining light' of the Messiah. Indeed, Israel is destined to be the catalyst of universal redemption – by example and by precept.

In turn, Israel itself will reach its full spiritual destiny only when all wickedness will vanish like smoke and 'the dominion of arrogance will pass away from the earth,' and people of righteousness and piety will triumph. In the final analysis, redemption – universal and national – requires man's conquest of evil, individually and collectively.

This lofty vision inspires our proclamation of God's holiness during the *Yamim Nora'im* – the High Holydays.

SERMONS

II
Sermons
ראש השנה
Rosh Hashanah

1. The Blessings of Fear*

> Shall the Shofar be blown in a city, and the people not tremble?
> Shall evil befall a city, and the Lord hath not done it?
> The lion hath roared, who will not fear?[1]

This Rosh Hashanah we need no *Machzor* to remind us that a great judgment is at hand – that the fate of humanity is in the balance. In former years we may have required some imagination or pure faith to believe that on these Days of Awe all mankind, every human being, is being judged for life or for death. Today our daily newspapers report the awful warnings of doom and destruction found in our sacred liturgy: – '**And Thou openeth the Book of Remembrance, and it reads by itself.**' The records are open, the facts proclaim themselves. Looking down at our stricken planet threatened with a calamity of universal proportions, '**even the angels are terrorized, seized by fear and trembling.**'

At this supremely critical moment no faith is needed to convince us that right now decisions are being made not merely on the issue of peace or war, but *mi yichyeh umi yamuth*, on the very survival or extinction of man; *mi ba'esh*, whether by the searing fire of atomic radiation, *umi bamayim*, or by hydrogen blast, *mi bara'ash*, whether by the artificial

---

*The first two of five addresses on the fundamentals of Judaism, delivered at the Fifth Avenue Synagogue, New York, during the High Holydays 5722–1961, when the Berlin Crisis, and the resultant tension between East and West, was at its height.

earthquake of a multi-megaton bomb, *umi bamagephah*, or by the plague of bacteriological warfare.

These are grave times. Charged to proclaim the word of God and to offer you His guidance in this period of peril and perplexity, I face a crushingly heavy responsibility. In the poet's stirring words we heard this morning in our *Shacharit* service:

> My heart grows hot the while I muse and pray,
> 'Tis kindled as a fiery glowing coal;
> Doubts, like a tempest, agitate my soul;
> For terror hath invaded us this day.

This is not the time for entertaining sermons. On these Days of Judgement, I propose not to preach, but to reason with you. The time at my disposal on a single day is too short to develop the momentous subject of man's judgment. Consequently, I will divide my talk into two parts, dealing today with the challenge, and tomorrow and on Yom Kippur with our response. During the precious hours of our devotions before God we have some hard work to do together, you and I. My task is to guide you in this work; yours to respond and co-operate with me.

I stand, as some of you may, utterly perplexed before one of the greatest riddles of all times. Here the world's leading statesmen glibly and almost casually brandish the threat of thermo-nuclear warfare, which could well reduce one-half of mankind to charred bone fragments, and the other to demented cripples. Here we live at the brink of history's deepest abyss, at the capricious mercy of some power-drunk leader, who cares neither for God nor for human life, who would willingly and without any scruples sacrifice hundreds of millions on the altar of his political ambitions, and who need only order the push of one button to obliterate, minutes later, a super-city like New York so completely, that the lava-strewn ruins of ancient Pompey would look like Paradise by comparison. And yet with such diabolical devastation and universal agony staring us in the face – tomorrow or next year or the year after – we somehow remain unperturbed, relatively indifferent to our fate.

Outside the most ominous and tempestuous clouds of war ever to appear on earth are visibly gathering, while inside us there is calm, not like the calm before the storm, but in truth the calm in the hurricane's eye.

I feel this uncanny contrast within myself, and I am shocked by it, and I see it in others around me. We all carry on our lives more or less as if we were on a pleasure cruise on some distant planet.

But this is not the whole point of my riddle.

Imagine the proposed target of a devastating attack were not the whole of humanity nor even all of the United States, but just the Jewish people. Imagine some gangster with the most powerful forces at his command would threaten to drop bombs on all Jewish centres, wipe out all Jewish areas, shoot at Jewish families wherever they were found.

What consternation, what an outcry, what terror there would be!

Would we not, if we could do nothing else, proclaim fast-days and hold special services of intercession which would be packed to capacity from morning to evening every day? Would there be a single Jew who would not readily give up his business or pleasure any hour of the day or night to storm the barriers between us and God and plead for mercy? Would that not be a natural instinctive reaction of a people to a forewarning of impending slaughter?

But once the assault is aimed at all citizens of the world, not just at one selected community, we seem composed and little agitated.

Let me develop this question one step further.

Imagine you or I had a child that was very sick, and the doctors said it might die or remain a cripple for life. Could we forget that worry for a single moment? Would not the very contours of our faces betray our grave anxiety and despair?

And even if the doctors had given up hope and we ourselves could give no medical aid to our stricken child, would we not at least pray, and pray with utter devotion for the child's safe deliverance, so that we would have the satisfaction – if nothing else – of at least having done something to stave off such a tragedy? And when, under the burden of such a peril, we prayed for our child, would we not weep bitterly until our faces were swollen with tears and all other thoughts banished from our mind? Would that not be a perfectly normal reaction?

Yet, when this tragedy threatens not only some child – yours or mine – but all of us, it leaves us comparatively unaffected.

Should one not expect at a time like this that rivers of tears would flow in our synagogue, that frantic screams for help would accompany our prayers, that a stampede of worshippers would crush the very walls of our houses of worship?

Should one not expect that, stirred and chastened by the experience of having such a ghastly fate hanging over our heads, everyone of us, you and I, would become a little more serious and responsible in our daily conduct, that this overwhelming pressure on our conscience would find some constructive outlet and produce some tangible changes in our lives? Would you not be entitled to expect of a person like myself to study a little more every day, of how our Prophets and Sages faced up to disaster, so that I might be more inspired by their lessons and inspire others as well? Would I not be entitled, conversely, to expect of individuals who might hitherto have been somewhat indifferent, to our dietary laws, for example, to resolve in this supreme emergency to uphold the Divine laws of *Kashrut* in and outside the home; or others who might have spent more on entertainment than on charity, to decide in future to respond to the cries of the needy according to their means? In short, should we not expect in these terror-ridden times that everyone would feel the urge to eliminate some of his shortcomings and to demonstrate some token of genuine repentance, even if only on the off-chance that perhaps a return to God might avert the evil decree?

Is it credible, then, that in fact nothing of such a spirit of contrition is to be seen, that on the contrary some people seem to worry more about what synagogue seat is allocated to them than about the prospect of themselves and their seat being blown to bits? Is it thinkable that while threatened with such a ghoulish massacre anybody can still give a thought to petty trifles?

Now let me ask: If you saw parents whose child was critically ill, and these parents faced the prospect of the child's death or mutilation with complete abandon and equanimity – would you not say that such parents were unfit to have the child, and deserving of what was coming to them?

Shall it be said of our generation that, if we are so unconcerned with our fate as to carry on life as usual, if in facing danger we still refuse to seek God and to pray to Him every day, that we deserve what is coming to us?

For *one* life in danger our heart would bleed, and for *millions* in danger our heart is impervious to all feelings. How can one explain this? Have we really become so callous, have we already lost our senses, our humanity, so completely that we care less about the destruction of all mankind, including ourselves and our children, than the loss of a single child? What is the answer to this riddle?

Evidently the magnitude of the threatened disaster simply staggers the human mind, stuns our senses and blunts our feelings. A Hebrew proverb says: *Tzaroth rabbim chatzi nechamah*, 'Trouble shared by many is half the consolation.' Perhaps, therefore, *Tzaroth kulanu kol nechamah*, 'Trouble shared by all is the whole consolation.'

I can find no other explanation for this inconsistency except that it is one of the most distressing limitations of our mind and heart, apparently a failing with which we are born.

Maybe this explains the Jewish emphasis on individuals, on single lives, in the creation both of humanity and of the Jewish people. Had Judaism taught that God created millions at the beginning, human life would have been without value: 'Therefore a single human being was created at first,' says the Mishnah **'to teach you that whoever destroys one life is as if he destroyed a whole world**.'[2]

The same applies to the origins of our people. Our history, in contrast to that of other peoples, did not begin with the emergence of a whole nation, nor even a tribe, but with single individuals, with the Patriarchs. Their example has set the values and inspired the lives of the Jewish people throughout our history for the very reason that our attention is focused on single personalities and not on a multitude.

That was also the greatest value of the Eichmann trial. The tragedy of six million dead moved us less, with all the harrowing stories and pictures in the newspapers, than the personal accounts of a few wretched survivors who reduced the tragedy to individual persons in the witness box. Millions mean little to us; individuals mean everything.

Our first task, then, is to think of the *olam maleh* 'the whole world', in terms of *nefesh achath*, 'a single life', to individualize the danger facing us. Then we may begin to feel the pain and the agony and the terror of the situation.

For pain and adversity, too, may be a blessing. If decaying teeth would not ache us, we would never go to the dentist, to have them repaired. If acute appendicitis were painless we would never consult the surgeon and have the diseased organ removed before it bursts with its lethal contents. Instead of living with pain, we would die without pain. Pain saves lives.

Maybe if we really felt some excruciating pain from the disaster hanging over us, we would turn to the Healer of all flesh and still save our lives.

We are about to hear the shrill sounds of the *Shofar*, the siren that served as a warning signal in the far past. 'Shall the Shofar be blown in a city, and the people not tremble?' Let it shake us out of our lethargy, let it make us tremble in fear and awaken us to the reality of our situation. The fear of danger is the greatest protection against it. 'When the lion roars, who will not fear?' The man who is not afraid of lions will much sooner be mauled and devoured than the one who fears its violence.

But pain and fear are merely negative reactions. Today we have dealt with the challenge. *Machar yihyeh ha'oth hazeh* – tomorrow we shall begin to discuss our response to it.

Meanwhile let me conclude with Hillel's immortal counsel: **'If I do not care for my own life, who will? And if I care only for myself, what am I? And if not now in this supreme crisis, when?'** *Yehi ratzon shetithchadesh alenu shanah tovah umethukah*, 'May it be God's will to renew unto us a good and sweet year.'

2. 'With All Thine Heart' – The Meaning of Prayer*

> And repentance and prayer and righteousness avert the evil decree.
>
> (*High Festival liturgy*)

Yesterday we considered our reactions and feelings in the face of the present grave threat to the peace of the world and to the survival of mankind.

You may now ask: 'Of what use and advantage is it even if we are aware of the danger? What can we do, when we are so completely impotent and defenceless? We cannot even build an ark like Noah to ride over the waves of destruction.' The only really effective defense against modern warfare – as against cancer or heart-attack – is prevention.

As Jews we cannot contribute atom-bombs or rockets to the defence of peace. 'Some trust in chariots and some in horses; but we will make mention of the Name of the Lord our God.'[3] Our principal weapon is prayer. When Jacob rescued his children from danger 'with my sword and with my bow,'[4] the *Targum* renders these words *Bitzlothi uvera'uthi*, 'with my prayers and my supplications.'

So long as we believe that the world is not governed by some blind forces of mechanical determinism, so long as we do not surrender to the idolatry of fatalism but affirm that there is a God who rules and guides our destiny, we must believe in the supreme power of prayer.

If you did not believe in the efficacy of prayer, you would not be at synagogue today. As soon as one abandons the belief in prayer, religion becomes an empty pretense, Judaism collapses.

---

*The second address on the fundamentals of Judaism, delivered at the Fifth Avenue Synagogue, New York, during the High Holydays, 5722–1961.

The synagogues would then better serve as temples of truth if converted into laboratories of science, and our Holy Arks should be filled with test-tubes rather than with sacred scrolls.

But the power of prayer depends upon the energy we put into it, just like the strength of a battery corresponds to the electric energy with which it has been charged. Can we supply this invincible power to our prayers?

Let me read to you the following pertinent observation of my revered father-in-law in the very opening sentences of his book *The World of Prayer*:

> Modern man has lost the capacity to pray. Rare indeed are the individuals who can free their souls from the paralyzing apathy of our days…from the disastrous spell of rationalism and materialistic thought, to pray with deep devotion for the realization of the ultimate purpose in life. The worshipper is conscious neither of the comforting and purifying power of prayer nor of its elevating and ennobling effects, for prayer fell victim to a culture estranged from God and became degraded to an act of mere habit.[5]

Real prayer requires anguish, a feeling of inadequacy and nothingness in relation to God, a shaken soul, a bleeding heart. '**The Lord is near unto them that are of a broken heart, and such as are broken in spirit He saves**.'[6] Thus the Psalmist speaks of 'The prayer of the poor man.'[7] This aspect of prayer is so vital that Jewish law, in a truly poignant regulation, requires of the *Chazan*, of the Reader who leads the congregation in prayer, 'that he shall be married and have children, so that he shall [know how to] pour out his heart and offer supplications from the depth of his heart.'[8]

Perhaps our lives today are too easy to appreciate the essence of prayer. Thank God, we do not know what it means to suffer hunger, to worry whence to take tomorrow's bread for our children, to run to the synagogue on *Shabbat mevorchin* preceding the new month and cry out for a *chayim shel parnasah*, 'a life of sustenance.'

We must learn again how to *daven*; how to pray properly.

There is a story of a Chasid in distress who went to his Rebbe and asked him to intercede with God on his behalf. 'Rather than ask me to pray for you,' countered the Rebbe, 'why don't you ask me to teach you how to pray, so that you can address your pleas to God yourself?'[9]

Alas, I can neither pray for you nor teach you how to pray, I have to learn that great art myself. Let us try together, then, and study how to pray from the teachings of our faith.

Adversity itself is the best teacher. A remarkable Midrash on our biblical Rosh Hashanah readings says: 'Why were our Matriarchs, the mothers of our people, barren for so long? Because the Holy one, blessed be He, desired to hear their prayers.'[10] Did our rabbis really mean to suggest that God inflicted the agony of childlessness on these righteous women simply because He loved to hear them cry and plead? What sort of pleasure did God have in seeing Sarah wait desperately for the blessing of maternity until she was ninety years old, or Rachel utter her anguish *cri de coeur* 'Give me children, or else I die,'[11] or Hannah weep sorely 'in bitterness of soul'[12] for the gift of a child?

No, the meaning of the Midrash is that God wanted to teach them how to pray. He yearned for the kind of prayer which can come out of the depths of affliction. Moreover, our Sages averred that it was on Rosh Hashanah that these three women received the promise of motherhood.[13] For it was on Rosh Hashanah, our rabbis surmised, that their prayers reached their climax. Historic men in Israel like Isaac, Joseph and Samuel are born only to parents who pray for their children with the soul-stirring fervour and desperate urgency shown by these women. That is what God craved for.

But to reach that climax in prayer on Rosh Hashanah is possible only after long and regular practice. These noble women had prayed on other days, too. They had pleaded God every day of the year, even if He answered them only on Rosh Hashanah.

A man who uses his legs only three times a year will find that he cannot walk properly even then, for his muscles will waste for lack of exercise. Similarly, he who prays only on Rosh Hashanah and Yom Kippur may find his prayers limping even on these days. Prayer requires constant exercise to be effective.

Next, prayer needs intense concentration. In the beautiful words of the Talmud, '**A man's prayer is not heard unless he offers his soul with it**.'[14] The great Rabbi Nachman of Bratzlav, grandson of the founder of Chasidism, paraphrased these words thus: '**Man must lose himself in prayer and forget his own existence**.'[15]

Our Sages spoke of prayer as *avodah shebelev*, as 'a service or labour of the heart.'[16] Prayer to them meant hard work and heart-work; and a heart operation is a most delicate operation. Now imagine a heart-surgeon bending over his patient during a cardiac operation and thinking not of his work but of the fees due him the day before which did not come in. Similarly the worshipper who, while attending a Divine service, puts his mind on business matters instead of on his prayers in single-minded devotion. As a famous seventeenth-century Polish preacher expressed it so felicitously: '**Is this a service of the heart, when the body is in the synagogue and the mind in the market**?'[17]

Prayer must spring from, and produce, a mood of ecstasy. Listen to this meaningful analogy drawn by the Baal Shem Tov: 'When a person is drowning in a river and he struggles with violent motions to save his life, surely his onlookers would not laugh at him. So also, if a man prays and shakes his body whilst doing so, one should not ridicule him, for he tries to save himself from the turbulent waters of distraction which seek to divert his mind from his prayers.'[18]

True prayer enlists the heart more than the brain; even the illiterate can pray with the deepest devotion. The story is told of a simple peasant who appeared before the Baal Shem Tov (the founder of Chasidism) soon after the conclusion of Yom Kippur grief-stricken that he could not join the congregation in prayer on the holy day. In weeping tones he told the great Rebbe that, as he was about to close his little store and go on his way on the eve of Yom Kippur, he was held up by some officials who engaged him until nightfall, forcing him to spend the holy day in his village which had no *minyan*. He had no *Machzor*, nor could he read anything except the letters of the *Aleph-Beth*. Thus he sat all day broken-hearted going over the Hebrew alphabet and hoping that God would order his disjointed letters into prayers. How could he now atone for his absence from the synagogue on Yom Kippur? After listening to his tale of woe, the Baal Shem Tov placed his hands on the head of his petitioner and exclaimed: 'For the past ten years no prayer as beautiful and pure as yours has ascended to Heaven.'[19]

This, then, is the road of prayer. Where does it lead? What will it achieve?

To begin with, prayer strengthens us to bear our burdens and to persevere in adversity. In the touching words of the famed Yiddish writer Peretz: 'Prayer sometimes dulls the hunger of the pauper, like a mother's finger thrust into the mouth of her starving baby.'[20]

But prayer does more than act as a palliative. Genuine prayers are answered, too. Who has not had some experience, at one time or another, of a miracle being wrought by prayer? Let me relate my own personal experience. During my ten years in Ireland, there were three occasions, and only three occasions, when we publicly recited *Tehillim* (Psalms) for desperately ill patients. The first time it was an old man, devout and beloved by the community. He was sinking fast, and the doctors had given up all hope for his recovery. One morning, in our despair, we called the congregation together and implored God in readings from the Psalms to spare this wonderful man's life. From that very day the tide began to turn; he rallied and recovered miraculously.

Another occasion concerned a young girl, a pupil of our Talmud Torah. She had been struck by a severe attack of polio. Placed in an oxygen tent, her life ebbed visibly. The doctors told the grief-stricken parents to be prepared for the worst. Once more the congregation gathered to say *Tehillim*. Defying the medical prognosis she suddenly regained her strength and she was back at our school a few months later.

The third time it was my own child, then a few-months-old baby. Dehydrated and emaciated to her little bones, she was rushed to the hospital in a pitiful state. The doctors' hopes faded as she would not respond to treatment. At the height of the crisis my friends joined in a heart-rending plea for mercy by reciting *Tehillim* together at the end of our *Shacharit* Service. The child, snatched from the Angel of Death by prayer, is in your midst today to tell the happy ending of this story.

I am by training and temperament too much of a rationalist to be usually given to mystic beliefs, and I would not relate such incidents to you if I had not been a personal witness to them.

Prayer can save not only individuals but also vast cities. The final biblical lesson we shall read on these Days of Awe is the Book of Jonah. It tells the story of an historic deliverance by prayer so topical, so exciting and so dramatic that I shall read the account of its climax to you:

> And the word of the Lord came unto Jonah the second time, saying: 'Arise, go unto Nineveh, the great city, and make unto it the proclamation that I bid you.' So Jonah arose, and went unto Nineveh, according to the word of the Lord. Now Nineveh was an exceeding great city, of three days' journey. And Jonah began to enter into the city a day's journey, and he proclaimed, and said: 'Yet forty days, and Nineveh shall be overthrown.'

> And the people of Nineveh believed God; and they proclaimed a fast, and put on sackcloth, from the greatest of them even unto the least of them. And the tidings reached the king of Nineveh, and he arose from his throne, and he laid his robe from him, and he covered him with sackcloth, and he sat in ashes. And he caused it to be proclaimed and published through Nineveh by the decree of the king and his nobles, saying: 'Let neither man nor beast, herd nor flock, taste anything: let them not feed, nor drink water; but let them be covered with sackcloth, both man and beast, and let them cry mightily unto God; yea, let them turn every one from his evil way, and from the violence that is in their hands. Who knows whether God will not turn and repent, and turn away from His fierce anger, that we perish not?'

> And God saw their works, that they turned from their evil way; and God repented of the evil which He said He would do unto them; and He did it not.[21]

The present-day Nineveh covers the entire world, all men and all beasts. To avert our doom let us Jews, as the Prophets of mankind and the Kingdom of Priests, arouse humanity to cry mightily unto God, to plead for peace with every ounce of our strength we can muster, so that our Father of mercy may have pity over His creatures and turn away from His fierce anger to grant us the supreme blessings of life and tranquillity.

3. The Human Rights Revolution*

Among the convulsions that have changed the face of our post-war world few are more thrilling and dramatic than the revolutionary movements in quest of human equality.

Throughout history, mankind has been divided into ruling peoples and subjugated peoples, empires and colonies, masters and slaves.

Now, within only 20 eventful years, all this has radically changed. The drive for equality has become the most potent social and political force of our times, perhaps of all times.

Scores of nations, even in the world's darkest and longest-dominated regions, have suddenly thrown off the shackles of colonialism and have been raised to independence, ranking as equals in the family of nations with countries as powerful as the United States or Great Britain.

At the same time, our country is astir with the cries of millions of disenfranchised citizens demanding equality in status, in opportunity, in education and in jobs.

---

*The first of five addresses delivered at the Fifth Avenue Synagogue, New York, during the High Holydays, 5724-1963.

These momentous developments may well mark one of the most decisive and constructive turning points in the history of human relations.

To Jews this historic turn of events should occasion special rejoicing and gratification, and particularly on Rosh Hashanah, man's birthday. For the subject of equal rights for all men as children of God created in His image is the historical significance and major theme of this festival. We celebrate today the 5724th anniversary of the brotherhood of man!

It was, after all, our Prophets who proclaimed thousands of years ago the doctrine of the unity of man, when it was still unheard of among the peoples of the earth: 'Have we not all one father? Hath not one God created us? Why do we deal treacherously every man against his brother, profaning the covenant of our fathers?'[22]

We have recently witnessed the March on Washington, the first mass demonstration for human equality ever held. We Jews have marched on our synagogues for countless centuries, every year, every Rosh Hashanah and Yom Kippur, to hold demonstrations for human equality. Our people, our saints and our sinners, men, women, and children, have for millennia past dreamt and prayed for the day when, in the exalted words of our festival liturgy: '…all humans shall form one band to perform Thy will with a perfect heart.' We have proclaimed annually for many centuries at our most solemn services: 'And all believe that He is soft to reconcile, the Great Leveller Who renders equal the small and the great.'

What is happening today represents the greatest and most universal consummation of Jewish ideals, the most dramatic realization of Jewish teachings, brought to the world by a hundred generations of Jewish history and cultural pioneering.

We can appreciate how distinctly Jewish this concept is when we contrast conditions here with those in Israel. More has been achieved in one decade in Israel to integrate the most diverse cultural elements – white with coloured, untutored with highly educated immigrants, than has been accomplished here in a century! In Israel no police force is required to secure the admission of dark Yemenite or Moroccan children to schools; no citizen is debarred from houses of worship, or denied his right to vote. None is segregated in public or private places because of his colour; whereas here and in South Africa, governors and governments, churches and universities are still in the forefront of the losing battle to maintain segregation and apartheid.

But why travel so far across the nation to the Deep South, or across the Atlantic to a distant land? Right here, next door, in my own apartment building, and presumably in many others in my own apartment building, and presumably in many others in the neighbourhood, coloured people are still forbidden to ride in the front elevator, unless saved from their degradation by the company of a white child!

The great revolution, then, has only begun, and it may yet take decades or generations until it is completed. For this is necessarily a slow and painful process which cannot be successfully accomplished overnight in the fact of eons of prejudice, ignorance, hatred, and cultural cleavages.

What is needed is infinite patience no less than vision and fortitude until all men will appreciate and cherish the supreme meaning of this day, expressed so profoundly in the Mishnah dealing with of the worth of every individual human being: *Lephichach nivrah adam yechidi...shelo yomar adam lechavero abba gadol me'avicha,* '**Therefore was man originally created as a single being...that no man should say to his fellow "My father is greater than yours"**.'[23]

This classic statement epitomizes the characteristic difference which still distinguishes the Jewish position from that of our civil rights movements and from the popular attitude in general. Our ideal is that no man should say to his neighbour 'My father is greater than yours.' It does not state that only one human being was created as the progenitor of all mankind in order that every man may claim 'My father is *as great as* yours,' but rather that people shall *not claim* 'My father is *greater than* yours.'

In other words, it is not the one who feels *inferior* who shall *claim* equality, but the one who feels *superior* who shall *grant* equality. The emphasis is on respecting the equal status of your neighbour, and not on his right to demand equal status with you.

In Jewish thought, we never speak of human rights, only of human duties. We list the teachings of Judaism as *Mitzvoth*, as commandments, not as *zechuyoth*, as rights. We put the onus of righteousness on the giver, not the taker. We teach people not to think in terms of what they may *demand from others*, but of what they *owe to others*. Here lies exposed one of the main curses afflicting our age: people talk more of rights than of duties; they are concerned more with what they can get out of life than what they have to put into life. Even in Jewish congregations there are many who are interested more in what the synagogue should do for them than in what they should do for it.

Judaism teaches that we cannot enjoy any privileges until we first attend to our obligations, that human rights will not be a universal reality until we first think and act on our human duties.

With all our enthusiastic espousal of human equality, however, we must recognize that there is also a negative side to this ideal. To exaggerate the scope of equality is as dangerous as to minimize it. Indeed, a distorted over-emphasis on human equality may well be the cause of some of the great problems facing our society.

The very Mishnah which posits the equal status of all men as the reason for the creation of a single human being in the beginning, also utilizes this fact to teach the infinite variety of men: 'And therefore man was originally created as a single being...to tell the greatness of the Holy One, blessed be He; for if man strikes many coins from one die, they are all equal to each other, but the King of Kings moulded all humans from the die of the first man (Adam), and yet not one of them is like his fellow.' While man-made articles mass-produced from a single prototype are all alike, God's creatures, though reproduced from a single individual, are all different. No two human beings are identical. The descent of all men from one common ancestor thus testifies, on the one hand, to the equal status enjoyed by all and, on the other hand, to the incomparable uniqueness of the Creator in making mankind so infinitely diverse that out of the billions of humans no two are alike.

There is no contradiction here. The two statements complement each other. All human beings *have* basically equal rights and equal duties. But they *are* not equal, nor are they meant to be. On the contrary, the miracle of creation is that no two people are alike. We are all different in looks, in disposition, in character and in intellect. The same applies to nations. No two of them are the same in their national characteristics, achievements and purposes.

This endless diversity is precisely the spice of life. Ludwig Boerne once said: '**Where only equals meet, boredom will soon preside, and stupidity will serve as secretary**'.

It is this diversity which, in our misplaced overexuberance for human equality, is bound to give way under the inexorable pressure of the steamroller of uniformity. Such misguided addiction to equality expresses itself, particularly in America, in many forms – from such trivia, say, as fashions, to fundamentals, as school education.

Let some celebrity start a new fad or fashion, and everybody will want to copy it, until all look alike like a row of ninepins.

Again, at the other end of the scale of values, many of our most powerful personalities and organizations are committed to the shallow principle that all American children should be educated alike, that only the uniform type of public schools should be deemed legitimate and deserving of state support.

Instead of giving people equal rights and duties, they want to *make* everyone equal, shape them all alike, put them all in the Procrustean bed of conformity and dull monotony.

A passage in the Talmud declares: 'Jerusalem was destroyed only because they made equal the small and the great, as it is written "and it is like people, like priest".'[24] This perverted doctrine of equality – seeing to level out all differences, making alike the great and the small, priest and people, leader and follower, saint and sinner, one religion and another – was responsible, according to our Sages, for the decline and fall of Jerusalem!

A society raised along one pattern is as prone to collapse as a building erected on a single pillar, and as useless as a machine made only of equal parts.

Scientific support for this fundamental point was only recently discovered and underscored. At the International Congress of Genetics an outstanding scientist-philosopher urged that greater attention be paid human genetic diversity than to human equality. The report continued:

> As our understanding of genetics increases, we shall, I believe, see that society is freest in which opportunity for acting according to one's genotype (hereditary makeup) is maximized.
>
> He declared that no attempt had yet been made under either capitalism or socialism to place people in society so that they would be happiest and most efficient. One reason for this failure, he suggested, has been the preoccupation with asserting racial or national homogeneity and neglecting the fact of intrinsic human inequality.[25]

As Jews we have a special stake in seeing the desire for human diversity maintained and encouraged. We cannot preserve our identity and religious distinctiveness except in a society which looks on diversity not as a bane but as a boon, not as an impediment to national greatness but as an enrichment of national life.

We cannot be creative in an environment which regards swimming against the stream as unpatriotic. The right and willingness to be different are the very warp and woof in the fabric of Jewish survival.

We have already sacrificed millions who defected from traditional Judaism on the altar of conformity. We *want* equal obligations and privileges, but we do *not want to be* equal.

These two aspects of human equality and diversity make up the content of this festival's most superb prayer, the *Aleinu*, a prayer so fundamental and exquisite that it has been borrowed from the Rosh Hashanah liturgy to accompany us every day of the year as the concluding climax of all our services. This is the prayer with which countless Jewish martyrs throughout our history have gone to their death because they were denied equal *rights* and because they yet refused to *be* equal, insisting that to live a life like others was not worth living.

This noble prayer begins, *Aleinu leshabe'ach la'adon hakol*, with 'our duty to praise the Master of all,' to render thanks to Him *shelo asanu kegoyei ha'aratzoth velo samanu kemishpachoth ha'adamah*, 'for *not* having made us like the nations of other lands, and *not* placed us like unto others in the human family on earth,' acclaiming our Creator, *shelo sam chelkenu kahem*, 'for *not* having set our portion like theirs,' *vegoraleinu kechol hamonam*, '*nor* our lot like that of their multitudes.' For this favour we bend our knees and bow and thank God today and every day. We are happy and grateful for being different and distinct.

But at the same time *nekaveh lecha...lir'oth meherah*, 'we express the hope...that we may soon see' the acknowledgement by all men alike of their common duty *lethaken olam bemalchuth shady*, 'to establish the world under the Kingdom of the Almighty,' *vechol bnei basar yikr'u bishmecha*, 'when all the children of flesh will call upon Thy Name,' *yakiru veyed'u kol yoshvei tevel ki lecha tichra kol berech tishava kol lashon*, 'when *all* the inhabitants of the world shall recognize and know that unto Thee every knee must bend, every tongue must swear.'

Then, and only then, through diversity of life and unity of purpose, will the day dawn when *vehayah Hashem lemelech al kol ha'aretz bayom hahu yiheyeh Hashem echad ushemo echad*, '**the Lord shall be King over *all* the earth, in that day shall the Lord be One and His Name be One**.'

4. 'For Man is Born to Labour'*

'For man is born to labour...'[26]

The unusual plethora of empty seats this Rosh Hashanah proclaims the early timing of the festival and its rare coincidence with Labour Day, a coincidence which has not happened since 1937 and which will not occur again for the rest of this century. This combination not only deserves a sermon; it is a sermon in itself.

For us every Rosh Hashanah is Labour Day. The Hebrew *avodah*, 'labour,' also means 'service,' 'worship.' Celebrating the completion of God's labour in creating the world, we turn to the challenge of man's labour in perfecting the Divine order.

Judaism is particularly fond of this term *avodah*, work, labour, service, and its derivatives *eved*, 'servant,' 'worker,' and *avad*, 'to labour,' 'to serve.'

At the very beginning of human history God placed man 'into the Garden of Eden to work and to guard it.'[27] In the Jewish view, even paradise is a place for work. The only fit place for idleness is the cemetery.

The highest rank that the Bible can confer on man is *eved Hashem*, 'servant of the Lord.' It was applied to Moses and to the people of Israel. And the holiest ritual in the Temple at Jerusalem was called the *avodah*, 'the service,' 'the act of labour.'

Indeed, Jewish thought views the relationship between God and man as that of master and worker, employer and employee, as expressed in the famous passage of *Pirkei Avoth*, which may well represent the message of Rosh Hashanah: **The day is short, and the work is much, and the labourers are**

---

*The first of five addresses delivered at the Fifth Avenue Synagogue, New York, during the High Holydays, 5725-1964.

sluggish and the reward is great, and the Master of the house is urgent.'[28]

Rosh Hashanah is the day when our contract with God, our Employer, comes up for renewal. What are the terms of this contract which we negotiate every year at our High Holyday services?

First, 'the day is short.' Our working hours are all too short. We often wished they were longer. We ask for overtime: *zochreinu lechayim*, we want more life, longer employment. But at least while we are employed, time is the one gift we all share equally. During the year we may have had different earnings, we may have experienced varied fortunes or misfortunes; but time we all had in the same measure. Everyone of us is exactly one year older since last Rosh Hashanah. No one had one hour more or one hour less than anybody else.

Where we differ is how we have used this time, what we have accomplished during the year, what improvements we have made on ourselves and the world around us since last Rosh Hashanah.

The second clause in our contract provides, 'the work is much,' the tasks allocated to us are great indeed. God demands a full day's service every day. He has laid down duties to Him and to our family, to our fellow-Jews and to society at large, at home and in the synagogue, at work and even at leisure. He insists that we shall serve Him in all our activities. When we eat and drink, our motive should not be simply to gratify our appetite like the brute but to strengthen our body for the service of God, and when we go to sleep we are to think of bracing ourselves for the tasks of another day. Even when we enjoy the delights of marriage, our principal intention should be to become partners with God in the creation and perpetuation of human life.[29]

Our contract assures us 'the reward is great.' What other employer provides you with an income, with the air you breathe, the health you enjoy, and the very life that animates your body? What other boss can guarantee you, as part of your wages, peace of mind and happiness in life, the promise of immortality and a share in the making of history? Who else can give you the gift of children and the blessing of intelligence?

But, alas, 'the laborers are sluggish.' So many of us want to have a 'good time' rather than a useful time in life. We want more than lunch and coffee breaks during our working hours; we want to have time off from our duties to God in the evenings, on Sundays and other occasions. Sometimes we are not really at work even while attending services in the synagogue, but interrupt our spiritual labours by talking or just idling.

The contract states: 'the Master of the house is urgent.' He presses, He is in a hurry. He wants us to complete His plan for universal perfection. He needs our labour urgently. He has already waited over 5,000 years. Yet the job of achieving universal peace and human brotherhood is far from finished.

Think of the frustration of an architect who draws up a magnificent blueprint and provides all the materials for an architectural masterpiece, but whose workers are lazy and delay the execution of his plan from year to year.

Never for a single moment are we to forget the unfinished task of liberating the oppressed, of refining the conscience of man, of banishing violence and hatred, and making the pursuit of truth and virtue the highest ideal and fondest ambition of man.

We believe in collective bargaining. We belong to unions called congregations. We emphasize the value of collective worship.

We have come here today for public prayer, because we are convinced that the effect of an individual pleading with God on his own cannot be compared with a whole congregation pouring out their hearts together. Far more can be accomplished by collective supplication than by individual negotiations with God.

There is only one restriction: We cannot go on strike against God, our Employer. We can demonstrate, by all means. We can 'sit in' at His dwelling places, the synagogues, and unite to present our demands for 'a good life, for adequate sustenance, for redemption and salvation.' We can cry together, sing together and make all the noise we want to make our claims heard. As unions we can band together and appoint a spokesman, the *shali'ach tzibbur*, the public reader or messenger, who will plead and negotiate for us. But we cannot strike, lay down our tools, and allow human progress to come to a standstill.

Nor do we need to resort to strikes. For our Employer has promised to meet our demands if we fulfil His. As a labour union of workers in the vineyard of the Lord, we are even assured fringe benefits. W are to receive not only sickness benefits, but health insurance: '**And it shall come to pass, if ye hearken to these ordinances, and keep them, that the Lord thy God shall keep for thee the covenant and the mercy which He swore unto thy fathers...and the Lord will take away from thee all sickness...**'[30]

There is also the promise of superannuation: 'To love the Lord thy God, to hearken to His voice and to cleave to Him, for it is thy life and the length of thy days.'[31]

We are guaranteed not only holidays with pay, but holy-days with joy: '**And thou shalt rejoice in thy festival**.'[32]

Above all, our Employer has consented to let us, as His workers, share in the profits accruing to us from a moral, peaceful and happy world established according to His instructions.

In renewing, then, our contract with God today, let us pledge to carry out His assignments willingly and conscientiously, so that He, in turn, will inscribe us 'in the book of good life'.

5. The Scientific Revolution*

Of all the massive upheavals rocking our age, the scientific revolution is certainly the most spectacular. In historical perspective it may not prove to be the most momentous. The political, social and religious spasms of our time may well leave more lasting effects on the future history of mankind. Yet the exploits in science have captured our imagination most.

Characteristically enough, ours is an age designated, not by a political or social name, but by a scientific name. It is not called the Age of the United Nations, or the Age of Human Rights. The name is bears is the Atomic Age, the Space Age, or the Nuclear Age.

Our entire economy and social thinking are geared to science. We have crash programmes not to train wiser statesmen or better politicians, but to produce more and better scientists. We do not engage in international competitions to reduce crime or divorce rates, but in a race to the moon.

Some have compared the exploits of our age to the vainglorious pyramids the Egyptians built, and our astronauts to the gladiators of old, turning our world into a huge and expensive circus in which governments display breathtaking shows

---

*The second of five addresses delivered at the Fifth Avenue Synagogue, New York, during the High Holydays, 5724-1963.

and all humans are the thrilled spectators. And who knows whether, like the ancient pyramids and gladiators, our modern artifacts and actors will not also deal death and house the dead rather than assure and beautify life?

To religion, and to Judaism in particular, the spectacular rise of science is a matter of special concern.

There is no day more appropriate for discussing our relations with science, the study and exploitation of nature, than Rosh Hashanah. For *hayom harath olam*, 'this is the anniversary of the universe,' the birthday of nature, no less than *hayom ya'amid bamishpat kol yetzurei olamim*, 'the anniversary of man's birthday and his common origin,' about which we spoke yesterday.

As Jews we have never shied away from scientific inquiry or shunned the study of man and the universe. On the contrary, for us the pursuit of science became a religious precept: *Minayin shemitzvah al adam lachashov tekuphoth umazaloth, shene'emar ushmartem va'asithem ki hi chochmathchem uvinathchem le'einei ha'amim*, 'whence do we know that one is religiously obliged to conduct astronomical research? From the verse, **"For this is your wisdom and your understanding in the eyes of the nations"**.'[33] We value science so highly that we are required to recite a special benediction at the sight of an outstanding scholar or scientist, be he Jewish or non-Jewish: *Baruch…shenathan mechochmatho liberiyothav*, 'Blessed be He…Who gave of His wisdom to His creatures.'[34] Nature study is part of our religion, for it is the means by which to appreciate the grandeur of the Creator, even as we know the artist by his work: *Hashamayim mesaprim kevod keil*, 'The heavens declare the glory of God.'[35]

But modern science attempted more than just to investigate the laws of nature and harness them in the service of man. It became a rival and antagonist of religion. It pontificated on the origin and destiny of man with cock-sure confidence; it eliminated God, reduced man into a freak product of chance, and enthroned reason as the supreme deity. It spoke in accents of arrogance and with a finality and infallibility which even the most inspired Prophets never used. 'Science says' became the new dogma, replacing 'Thus sayeth the Lord.'

As a new philosophy of life, this worship of rationalism promised the millennium. In this vaunted age of rationalism, so its early devotees believed with a faith worthy of better causes, science would answer all questions; there would be no more wars, and the brotherhood of man would be a reality. Psychoanalysis would even rid us of all feelings of guilt and anxiety. Peace would rule inside and outside us.[36]

Alas, it did not work. The promises remained unfulfilled.

In a phrase we repeat constantly during this penitential season we say: *Sarnu mimitzvotecha umishpatecha hatovim velo shaveh lanu,* 'we have departed from Thy commandments and good laws, and it hath not profited us.' The flight from religion did not pay off.

Science has not removed the spectre of war, it has not reduced the divorce rate, it has not decreased crime and juvenile delinquency, it has not contributed to human happiness or security. Science has not proved a substitute for religion.

Perhaps this is just as well. If science had succeeded in making true its exaggerated claims as the panacea for all our ills, religion would have ceased to exist in the hearts of man.

Instead, religion has made an amazing come-back. Many of the nineteenth- and early twentieth-century apostles of science, who poured such scorn on religion, would turn in their graves if they knew how many of their dogmas have been debunked and how powerful religion is again after all its tribulations in the past 100 years.

Today science speaks in more humble tones. It knows it produced more questions than answers. What were once laws have become theories, and theories have turned into hypotheses. The ultimate mysteries of life and its meaning have not been unravelled; the limitations of science are today better realized than ever before.

The relationship between science and religion, between God's creation of matter and spirit, is well illustrated in a fascinating Midrash. When God created the world with words *Bereshith bara Elokim* ('In the beginning God created'), starting with the letter '*Beth*' – the second letter of the Hebrew alphabet, the first letter, '*Aleph*', complained: 'Why did You pass me over, creating the universe with the second letter instead of beginning the creation with me, the head of all letters?' But God reassured the '*Aleph*': 'By your life, your time will come; I have reserved for you an even greater act of Divine creation. For when I will reveal Myself at Sinai to proclaim the Ten Commandments, I will start with you: *Anochi Hashem*, ("I am the Lord, thy God").'[37]

What is the meaning of this apparently childish dialogue between God and a letter of the alphabet?

The Midrash teaches that the creation of heaven and earth, the wonders of nature with all its mysteries and unfathomable forces, the vastness of the universe and the marvels of the countless myriads of atoms composing it – all this is merely the 'B' of Divine creation. Greater and more wonderful still than any material creation, the 'A' and the primary demonstration of God's creativity, is what occurred at Sinai, when He proclaimed the purpose and meaning of everything He had called into existence, when He laid down the moral law which has to govern His creatures and make their lives worth living. Heaven and earth and all that fills them are only the means, the laws of nature reveal merely the secondary aspect of God's glory; the ultimate end is the fulfilment of God's will, the primary revelation of His majesty lies in the Torah, in the laws epitomized by the Ten Commandments, for the sake of which everything else was called into being and sustained in life.

Let us apply this supreme lesson to our own situation today. Let us translate this penetrating Midrash into contemporary terms.

We marvel today with boundless admiration at the ingenuity of the human intellect for its capacity to devise and construct a little sphere, hurl it into space and there make it travel on its predetermined orbit, girdling the globe at an incredible speed or hours, days or even years. If we marvel at that – as we should – what shall we say of an entire people which, over three thousand years ago, launched into the space of history ideas and ideals which continue to this day to orbit the earth, bringing not the threat of destruction, but inspiration, comfort, decency and holiness into millions of homes in every civilized country throughout the world, what shall we say of such a colossal achievement? We admire man's stupendous scientific and technological strides; but what are these compared to the gigantic efforts of a whole nation, through centuries of pioneering and martyrdom, to sustain and spread the ideals of morality, social justice and universal brotherhood, to devise and implement the one formula which has eluded all our scientists and technicians so far – how to build two homes next to each other so that peace will rule between them and harmony inside them?

What is demanded of our generation, if it is to restore its sense of values, is that in our dazzling admiration for our material and physical accomplishments we cease to be blinded to the incomparable achievements of the spirit, that we honour our saints and thinkers at least as much as our scientists and entertainers, that we recognize the primacy of the Ten Commandments in securing human peace and happiness over the countdowns of our rock-launches.

This is true relationship between spirit and matter, between man and machine, between moral power and physical force, is symbolized by the *Shofar* we are about to sound.

This *Shofar* is, admittedly, an ancient instrument. It is plain, natural and unsophisticated. There is nothing artificial about it. Nor has its shape or sound changed for millennia. Yet this simple little instrument has the power to summon more people together than all the greatest orchestras in the world combined. This humble *Shofar* can stir the conscience, move hearts, arouse us to our duties, more effectively than the most refined musical instrument invented by science.

What is the mystic power of the *Shofar*? What is its magnetic appeal outlasting the ages?

Its secret, like the secret of Judaism, is that it brings us the sounds of eternity.

It is the same ram's horn which marked the beginnings of Jewish history when Abraham substituted for his son on the altar a ram caught by its horns in the thicket. It is the same *Shofar* that our ancestors heard at Sinai to herald history's most momentous event. It is the same *Shofar* whose sounds rang through the halls of the Temple in Jerusalem. It is the same *Shofar* that sounded a warning signal whenever our people were in danger. It is the same *Shofar* which for thousands of years and for untold millions of Jews has given a foretaste of the *Shofar gadol*, the great horn, which would proclaim the time when: '**And it shall come to pass on that day, that a great horn shall be blown; and they shall come which were lost in the land of Assyria, and they that were outcasts in the land of Egypt; and they shall worship the Lord in the holy mountain at Jerusalem.**'[38]

יום כפור
Yom Kippur

1. 'With All Thy Mind' – Our Belief in God*

> And you shall love the Lord, your God, with all your heart, and with all your mind, and with all your means.[39]

Under the mounting stress of the present turbulent times I resolved this year to devote my addresses on these Days of Judgment to some of the fundamental teachings of Judaism rather than to any homiletical pleasantries. On Rosh Hashanah we discussed prayer which, together with repentance and righteousness, 'averts the evil decree'. Prayer is our response to the first call of the *Shema* – to love God with all our *heart*. On Rosh Hashanah we laboured with the heart; we exercised our emotions.

Tonight, at this most solemn service of the year, we shall deal with the first requirement for salvation; repentance, return to God, as our response to the second call of the *Shema*: to love God *bechol nafshecha*. This word in biblical Hebrew does not mean 'your soul' as it is usually rendered. It actually means 'your mind.' Thus the Book of Proverbs speaks of a *nefesh* without knowledge: *Gam b'lo da'ath nefesh lo tov*, which can only mean: 'Also, that the mind be without knowledge is not good.'[40] Again, the commandment to wear the *Tephillin* upon the arm and upon the head is introduced with the words:

---
*The third of five addresses delivered at the Fifth Avenue Synagogue, New York, High Holydays, 5722–1961.

'and you shall place these My words upon your heart (that is, facing the arm-*Tephillin*) and upon your mind.' *Nafshecha* must denote 'your brain' rather than 'your soul.'

According to Jewish law, the *Tephillin* of the head are more sacred than those of the arm or heart.[41] Paradoxical as it may sound, the heart of Judaism lies in the head. We rate Jewish thinking and Jewish knowledge even higher than Jewish feeling. Worse still than to be confined to a hospital is to be an inmate of a mental institution. There is no more precious possession than the health of the mind. Hence its spiritual welfare comes even before that of the heart in Judaism.

And so tonight we will put our brains to work; we will flex the muscles of the intellect, the mind, leaving the consideration of the third element, 'righteousness', performed 'with all our means' for tomorrow.

Return to God, that is to accept and love Him 'with all your mind,' means above all to acknowledge Him, to believe in Him. Now, the belief in God is by and large taken for granted, certainly among synagogue worshippers. What, then, is there to discuss on this subject?

But frankly, how deep and how widespread is this belief really today?

Let us first survey the belief in God on a universal scale. As God reviews this day the place of man on earth, let us review the place of God on earth. How has God's conquest of the human mind fared over the ages to the present time? The results of such a survey are not too reassuring.

There is taking place this day not only the opening of the General Assembly of the United Nations, a convocation of the leaders of peoples, but also a general assembly of all individuals populating the world to be mustered before God. As we shall read again tomorrow, 'And all that come into the world pass before You as sheep to be counted.'

In this 'general assembly' there are more than three billion people, divided almost equally into three camps; the religiously developed, the underveloped and the maldeveloped. Perhaps just over one billion people profess the monotheistic faiths of Judaism, Christianity and Islam. Another billion, spread over vast lands in Asia and the greater part of Africa, are religious neutrals, uncommitted, neither acknowledging nor rejecting God. Their religion differs little from the primitive notions of pagan antiquity.

And nearly another billion, alas, are in militant rebellion against God. Behind a curtain of iron they have built for themselves a mighty empire of science and materialism soaring into outer space, a gigantic edifice which makes the ancient Tower of Babel look puny by comparison. For the first time in history we have not only individuals but powerful states dedicated to the overthrow of all religion, states that seek to eradicate the belief in God from the hearts and minds of man as a matter of national policy. Such a *memsheleth zadon*, such 'a dominion of arrogance,' is entirely unprecedented in the annals of the human race.

Worse still, what the Western world refuses to recognize and what we Jews, who brought religion into the world, should be the loudest to proclaim, is that this is the crux of the ideological struggle between West and East. Instead of fighting phantoms – social doctrines or economic systems – we should above all attack the barbaric godlessness of our adversaries.

What we should never tire to consider is that communism as such teaches a lofty doctrine of human equality and brotherhood; a doctrine not entirely unrelated to our Prophets' passion for social justice. How can we explain, then, that communism has been perverted into such a diabolical instrument of oppression, that it has led to the rise of prisons engulfing almost whole continents, to the brutal destruction of all freedom, to the degradation of man into a soulless machine? How can fine ideals produce such a ghastly reality?

The answer is quite simple, apparently too obvious to be noticed: There can be no brotherhood of man without the Fatherhood of God. It is only as children of a common God that we humans are brothers. Take away the link, and the chain of human fraternity and understanding disintegrates. Dethrone God, and the dignity of man created in His image is bound to collapse. That is the true cause of all our present-day terror in the world.

Let us next examine the strength of the belief in God nearer home, in our own vaunted Judaeo-Christian civilization.

History appears to evolve in strange, uneven waves, in periodic cycles of ups and downs. The famous philosopher Whitehead asserted that the sum total of knowledge Europe had in the year 1500 was less than that possessed by the Greek scientist Archimedes in 212 BCE.[42] We may similarly discover that even in the West people know and care less about God in the twentieth century than they did 500 or 1,000 years ago.

In the past few centuries God has been on a massive, unparalleled retreat – and so has, not incidentally, human happiness and security. With all the rash of beautiful new synagogue and church buildings springing up everywhere, God matters less in modern society than ever before. People resort to religion as they do to tranquilizers – to drown their anxieties. They consult clergymen as they do a psychologist – to soothe neurotic minds or to eliminate deep-seated complexes. Religion has become another hunting ground for fun, happiness and entertainment or even fashion, instead of being the inspiration for the moral discipline of life it is meant to be.

Even here, in the very country which has as its motto 'In God We Trust', we live in an intellectual and cultural climate distinctly unfavourable to the healthy growth of religious beliefs and practices. Most American children spend more time every week in front of corrupting TV screens than on ennobling religious instruction; they know more about the ephemeral stars of Hollywood than about the immortal heroes of the Holy Land. Comics and science fiction are their new Bible.

The blame for this drift has often been laid at the door of science. It is alleged that in the light of our modern knowledge about the age of the world, the evolution of man, the insignificance of our planet in the vastness of space, one can no longer believe in a Creator, in Providence, in a Divine Law. How true is this charge? How objective are the findings of science, how unprejudiced its teachings and researches?

Listen to the illuminating words of one of the most eminent scientific writers of our country. Dealing with the unsolved riddle of evolution and discussing whether life could originally have created itself, he writes:

> The beginning of the evolutionary process raises a question which is as yet unanswerable. What was the origin of life on this planet? Until fairly recent times there was a pretty general belief in the occurrence of 'spontaneous generation.' It was supposed that lowly forms of life developed spontaneously from, for example, putrefying meat. But careful experiments, notably those of Pasteur, showed that this conclusion was due to imperfect observation, and it became an accepted doctrine that life never arises except from life. So far as actual evidence

> goes, this is still the only possible conclusion. But since it is a conclusion that seems to lead back to some supernatural creative act, it is a conclusion that scientific men find very difficult of acceptance. It carries with it, what are felt to be in the present mental climate, undesirable philosophical implications...For that reason most scientific men prefer to believe that life arose in some way not yet understood, from inorganic matter in accordance with the laws of physics and chemistry.[43]

'Undesirable philosophical implications' – there's the rub! What a devastating exposure of unscientific science! Scientific evidence honestly analyzed, it is admitted, points to God as the only reasonable and logical conclusion, yet it is 'difficult of acceptance,' for no other reason than giving some comfort and support to religious beliefs!

Where, then, I ask, is the real prejudice to be found today: with those who affirm the existence of God, and who have for so long been taunted with the charge of obscurantism and intellectual bias; or with 'scientific men,' who, while confessing that the conclusion of their observation leads to God, reject that conclusion because it does not fit into their preconceived notions of a Godless and soulless and meaningless nature?

Should we not, on the contrary, with all the awe-inspiring wonders and infinite marvels revealed by scientific researches, have a far more profound appreciation of God than the ancients?

Abraham had neither a telescope nor a microscope to peer into the mysteries of nature; yet he made the greatest discovery of all times, giving sense to life, meaning to existence, and purpose to history. He gazed at all the stars merely with the naked eye; yet of him it is written, 'And He (God) brought him outside and said: "Look now toward heaven, and count the stars…" And he believed in the Lord.' The Rabbis added a remarkable comment: 'God took Abraham outside the orbit of the world and lifted him above the stars' (Rashi), that is, Abraham's vision transcended the bounds of the finite universe to recognize the infinite God beyond.

Today we can increase our vision of nature by countless millions not only above us but also beneath. We are able not only to see galaxies at the unimaginable distance of 2,000 million light years and endorse with millions of proofs the proclamation of the Psalmist: 'The heavens declare the glory of God.'[44] We can also see the glory of God revealed in a tiny pin-head, with its considerably more than a million, million, million atoms, each of them a universe of its own.[45]

Why, then, does science fight shy of drawing the logical conclusion from its ever-growing accumulation of marvels? What accounts for its prejudice against religion? Why does science gain ever more devotees among our finest brains and religion lose them? Why do statements by leading scientists evoke greater respect than those of religious leaders?

The answer is simple: Science is impersonal and undemanding. It deals with things as they are, with life as it is; it wants nothing from us.

Religion, on the other hand, postulates ideals. It deals with things as they should be, with life as it ought to be lived; it points up the gap between what we are and what we should strive to become. It issues a personal challenge; it is exacting.

It is far easier to practice the religion of science than the science of religion. Science, it is hoped, will one day – if it does not destroy us before then – provide us with a life of perfect comfort and ease, rid us of all hard work and responsibilities. All we shall have to do is push buttons while sitting back in idleness to enjoy the pleasures of life in leisure unlimited.

Religion asks for the hard way, offering constant criticism and never permitting any self-satisfaction.

No wonder people prefer to worship the idol of science rather than the God of religion!

We have now surveyed the belief in God among humanity at large and society in general. Let us finally turn to ourselves.

To the Jewish people, after all, this belief is the very essence of our existence. In the celebrated words of Saadya Gaon, the first-ranking Jewish philosopher: **'Our nation is a nation only by virtue of its Torah.'**[46]

To begin with, our entire concept of the belief in God is different.

There is a story of a grandson of the famous Rabbi Akiva Eger – a pillar of the *Mithnagdim* – who was 'converted' to Chasidism. To imbibe the teachings of the new movement, he spent some time on a visit to the '*Chiddushei Harim*,' the renowned founder of the Gerer dynasty. On his return his father asked him: '*Nu*, what did you learn from the great Rebbe?' 'That there is a God,' was his cryptic reply. 'That even our non-Jewish maid affirms.' 'The difference is this,' he explained, 'she believes there is a God; I now know there is a God.'

The very term 'belief' is alien to Judaism. Our sacred writings speak of *da'ath Elokim*, 'the knowledge of God.'

To believe implies some doubt; to know is to accept a certainty. Religious belief is gained by intuition; knowledge by learning. Hence the Jewish emphasis on study, on constant learning. The way to the faith of Judaism leads primarily through the brain, not merely through the heart.

What sort of a God, then, is it we acknowledge and worship? Is it a God who is sovereign, independent, free and transcendent or a slave to the whims of man, subject to the dictates of our conscience?

We have today some large and powerful pseudo-religious movements founded on the premise that not everything in the Torah is Divine and eternal. Their theologians arrogate to themselves the right to discriminate between the laws of the Torah, picking and choosing what appeals to them and rejecting what they dislike. Ethical laws are fine and popular; these they accept as Divine. Ritual commandments are not attractive to their minds; these are consigned to the limbo of history as man-made and obsolete.

In other words, *they* decide what shall be law, not God. Their conscience makes the religion and dictates to God what shall be His will, using Him merely as a rubber stamp to confirm their notions of right and wrong. If the decision as to what our religion requires of us rests with them and not with God, why do they need God altogether? Their worship of the human conscience is idolatory, not religion; for their God is made in the image of man. He is a puppet whose strings are pulled by humans.

Our Prophets teach us to the contrary: '***He* declared unto you, O man, what is good and what the Lord seeks from you: Only to practice justice and the love of mercy, and to walk humbly with your God**.'[47] It is God who defines 'what is good,' not man.

The crux of our understanding of the knowledge of God lies in the last phrase, usually rendered 'to walk humbly with God.' Literally, the phrase has an entirely different meaning. The Hebrew word *hatzne'a* has the same root as *tzni'uth*, which denotes something hidden or secret. *Hatzne'a lecheth im elokecha* really means, therefore: 'To walk with your God even when you are in secret, quite alone with Him.'

The supreme test of our faith in God is not when we find ourselves assembled in the synagogue, but when we are alone with Him, when no one else watches.

In moments of grief and adversity, when we feel lonely and forsaken on the brink of despair, when we have been bereaved of a precious life near and dear to us, *then* to be comforted by His Presence and by His promise 'There will be hope for your future,'[48] *then* to vindicate His justice by proclaiming 'The Rock, perfect is His work'[49] and by reciting the *Kaddish* 'Sanctified and magnified be His Name...', thus 'to walk in loneliness with God' – that is *da'ath Elokim*, 'the knowledge of God'.

In times of temptation, when we find ourselves in secret places with the doors locked to the prying eyes of onlookers, on the verge of surrender to lust and sin, *then* to resist the overtures of passion, *then* to feel the heavy hand of shame lest we pollute ourselves, realizing that God is present – that is *da'ath Elokim*, 'the knowledge of God'.

When we are in business, and the opportunity knocks for some gain through a little fraud or dishonesty, even if no one could ever find out, *then* to be held back by the fear of Heaven – that is *da'ath Elokim*, 'the knowledge of God'.

The Hebrew word *da'ath* means more than mere intellectual knowledge. It also describes the most intimate relationship between husband and wife, as we read of the first humans: *Ve'adam yadah eth chavah ishto vatahar vateled*, 'And Adam *knew* Eve, his wife and she conceived and gave birth.'[50] Hence the Prophet speaks of the relationship between God and Israel in terms of: *Ve'erastich li...veyada'ath eth Hashem*, 'And I will betrothe you unto Me...and you shall *know* the Lord.'[51] We are to be bound to God with the same bonds of love and intimacy as unite married partners. And if a man really loves his wife, he will not be faithless to her even if his infidelity cannot be discovered; he will be loyal to her in secret as well as in public. That is what the true 'knowledge of God' requires of us.

That love, too, is mutual. God seeks our love: 'and you shall love the Lord, your God with all your heart...' In return He assures us of His love even before we recite the *Shema: Ahavah rabbah ahavtanu*, 'With abounding love have You loved us...'

On this supreme night, therefore, we plead with greater fervour and confidence than ever: 'As a father has compassion over his children, so may You, O Lord, have compassion over us!'

2. The Religious Revolution*

Having considered the human rights and scientific revolutions, we will now turn to the religious and moral upheavals of our contemporary society.

The businessman who may remain indifferent to the upturns and downturns in enterprises other than his own, will doubtless become intensely interested and personally involved in the security values affecting his own stock.

Our Jewish national business is religion and morality. They are the bread and water of our very existence. As we read in our prayers tonight and every night: 'For they are our life and the length of our days.' We should follow the fortunes of religion anywhere as we follow the ups and downs of stocks we own, for all our national wealth is invested in religion.

If to others, therefore, the religious revolution of our time may be of secondary interest, less exciting than the adventures in space and the crises in race, to us Jews the epoch-making

---

*The third of five addresses delivered at the Fifth Avenue Synagogue, New York, during the High Holydays, 5724–1963.

changes in the past 20 years in the affairs of religion in general, and Judaism in particular, must be the most dramatic and important events of our age.

These changes are certainly no less drastic and unprecedented than those which have swept away the pre-war notions of science and human relations. They are no less revolutionary.

Let me illustrate some of the most significant aspects of these changes by relating two stories of Rabbi Levi Yitzchak of Berditchev, the great Chasidic Rebbe of the eighteenth century who was a saint in his lifetime and became a legend in his death for his daring arguments with God in defense of Israel. The first story is based on the rabbinic law making it a special *Mitzvah* to eat and drink festively on Erev Yom Kippur just as it is our duty to fast on Yom Kippur.

It was on the Eve of the Holy Day. The congregation was assembled in the synagogues awaiting to hear the solemn chant of *Kol Nidrei*. Rabbi Levi Yitzchak was not in his customary seat. Holding a lit candle, the Rabbi was seen moving from bench to bench, as if in quest for something he might have lost...The worshippers, startled at this activity, asked their leader: 'Rabbi, what are you doing?' 'I have been looking for one inebriated Jew, but I find none.' Thereupon he ascended the pulpit and exclaimed:

> Lord of the Universe, who is like Your people Israel, chosen and holy? Where else would you find a people which, commanded to eat and drink, to feast a little more than usual, would not yield a single drunkard? Yet the ruling that an extra portion of food and drink should be consumed on the Eve of Yom Kippur yielded not one Jew who was soused. All partook of extra portions of food and beverages, after which they hastened to the synagogue. Not

one Jew is drunk or fatigued. All are sober and holy. All are ready for the pains of hunger and the privations of this sacred fast, willing to confess their sins before You and repent with a contrite heart. Surely they are worthy of Your forgiveness and to be inscribed in the Book of Life!

If we had a Rabbi Levi Yitzchak today, he might under different circumstances exclaim: Almighty God, take a look at Your unique people of Israel. Consider the immensity of the tragedy they had endured in the past generation. They were struck by the greatest of catastrophies ever to overwhelm any people. They lost six millions in history's worst slaughter. One-third of their entire people perished, the segment which represented our people's most fertile seed. With their death, the reservoirs of Jewish learning and piety were dried up and the strongholds of Jewish tradition wiped out.

Any other nation would have turned into an army of cynics and desperate radicals under the stress of such fearful blows. They would have lost faith in Divine justice, rebelled against a God Who betrayed them, and turned their back on a religion which should have disintegrated with the blood of its finest sons.

Yet the remnant of this people is tonight assembled by the millions in Your sanctuaries. There is not a Jewish community anywhere without a service to Your glory this night. What a people, what an indomitable faith, what a miracle of religious might!

And Rabbi Levi Yitzchak might have continued: Look at the Jewish people in the Western lands, especially in affluent America. Never before have Jews lived in such comfort and security. Never in history have they been exposed to such temptations to give up their ancient rituals and traditions, never have they been subjected to greater pressures of assimilation and conformity.

From within, dissident movements have been gnawing at the roots of the old tree, ready for the kill, confident that Orthodoxy could not survive. Already in 1924, a Reform Jewish magazine had declared: '...Orthodoxy in Judaism is something like snakes in Ireland...' They were convinced that the remnants of Torah Judaism would be swept away for good with the slums of the Lower East Side, especially once the supply of traditionalist immigrants from Europe was cut off for ever.

And now, look at the miracle of revival that has taken place. These 'doomed' traditionalists have made a fantastic comeback with a vengeance. Today Orthodox Jews are installed on Fifth Avenue hitherto a preserve for Reform Jews. They control virtually all Jewish day schools throughout the country. They raise tens of millions of dollars annually to sustain the most comprehensive system of Jewish education ever known in modern times, superior to anything seen in pre-war days. Today more than 60,000 American-Jewish boys and girls study Torah more intensively and for longer hours than any group of students pursue their studies at any university. We now have flourishing organizations of Orthodox scientists and Orthodox college students, units that scarcely existed ten or 20 years ago. Kosher meals are served increasingly in elegant hotels and to travellers on planes and ships – and, one hopes, soon even in Jewish hospitals. Despite our terrifying losses in Eastern Europe, the proportion of observant and learned Jews in the world today is probably as great as it ever was in modern times.

Two events during the past year highlight this amazing resurgence of traditional Judaism. One was the biggest mass-demonstration in tribute to a single Jew ever seen in America.

Tens of thousands of Jews, mostly young, massed in the streets of New York to bid farewell to the mortal remains of Rabbi Aaron Kotler זצ״ל, the foremost rabbinical Sage of our time. No Jewish leader, no Jewish statesman, philanthropist, nor the most popular Jewish celebrity or most outstanding Jewish scientist, ever received such honours. It was a manifestation of Orthodox strength which percolated into the daily press in long reports and impressive pictures the like of which had never been seen before.

The second event happened recently in Israel, where well-organized groups of young 'activists' staged simultaneous demonstrations in three cities against the missionary schools luring Jewish children from destitute homes away from our people and religion. We may or may not agree with the methods used, though we now know that, contrary to the tendentious newspaper reports, there was no violence of any kind. Nor was the action undertaken by 'fanatics,' as alleged. Mainly these were moderate students from the Zionist-oriented Yeshivoth. In any case, there is no Jew harbouring a spark of Yiddishkeit who did not leap with joy and pride that we still have in our midst doughty young Jews for whom *shemad,* apostasy, is the most horrifying word in the vocabulary, whose hearts bleed with grief and outrage at little Jewish children who, after having escaped from the clutches of persecution to find refuge in the Holy Land, are torn from their faith. It is a grim case of distress, poverty and ignorance being exploited for the purpose of spiritual kidnapping in their own land. We hear so much these days of the lost generation, about young Jews who do not care for the sanctities and beliefs of their people, who do not care for any Jewish values, and for whom neither intermarriage nor even *shemad* evokes any more the terror it did in the past. How great should be our joy, then, that we once more have young men who militantly defend our most precious possessions, and expose themselves to prosecution and humiliation in order to arouse the conscience of our people.

With the world-wide statistical increase of Orthodox Jews – resulting from a relatively high birth-rate, a low assimilation rate, and their massive conversion of other Jews – at many times the rate of the assimilationists, a new Rabbi Levi Yitzchak of Berditchev might soon take a candle in hand and crawl under the pews of our synagogue on Yom Kippur in a vain search for a non-observant Jew! Another 50 years, and with God's help we will be there!

This upsurge is not, of course, happening in a vacuum; it should be seen as part of the revolutionary changes in the religious patterns of society beyond our Jewish confines.

If it is one of the miracles of modern Jewish history that Judaism, instead of being smashed on the anvil of suffering and succumbing to the allurements of assimilation, has experienced a remarkable rebirth, it is no less of a miracle, in a world shaken to its foundations by two world wars, challenged by the new worship of money and science, assaulted by mighty empires of godlessness, that religion has survived altogether. It has survived, nay, it has even gained in strength. In past periods of such turmoil, history witnessed the rise of new religions, and the splintering or decay of old ones.

The opposite has now happened. Surprisingly, there are no signs of any new faiths and no further disintegration of the existing religions. Instead the old ones are drawn together; unity and dialogue are the great watchwords of our time. Different religions have begun to talk to each other; they seek common ground instead of battling one another. This is an altogether new phenomenon in the history of religion, a revolution if ever there was one.

Equally significant and epoch-making is the sudden end, in but 20 eventful years, of one religion as the dominant faith. After occupying for nearly 2,000 years a central and constantly expanding place in the political and cultural history of civilization, its dream of world conquest now appears at an end, following the liquidation of colonial empires and the suppression of missionary work in Africa and the greater part of Asia, not to mention the reverses behind the Iron and Bamboo Curtains. This, too, is a development of historic proportions, and with consequences to Jewish fortunes which are already beginning to be felt in the relaxation of 2,000 year-old tensions.

Following the old adage '*Wie es christelt sich, so juedelt's sich*,' we Jews have a vital stake in the religious loyalties of our non-Jewish neighbours. We are gratified, therefore, that religion in America, far from declining as a force in our national life, has lately come ever more to the fore. Where formerly religious items would be relegated to the back pages of our newspapers, they have recently often been front page news. Whether dealing with court decisions on religious issues or with reports on religious councils, they give a welcome indication that religion again begins to matter in the consciousness of the nation and the concern of its thinkers.

Our task is to nurture this consciousness and concern until the service of God will become the supreme pursuit of every human being as the fulfilment of our messianic aspirations. And the more devoutly religious our neighbours are, the more will Jews take their Judaism seriously.

But alas, this religious ferment also contains many bubbles of air. Let me now relate the second story of Rabbi Levi Yitzchak of Berditchev which, I believe, will illustrate the negative aspects of this religious awakening.

It happened one Rosh Hashanah. The Rebbe prepared himself for the blowing of the *Shofar*. He put on his *Kittel* (white gown), recited the stirring Psalm *Lamnatze'ach* seven times with the congregation, lifted the *Shofar* – and then suddenly stopped. The people waited, but there was no *Berachah,* no *Shofar* sound. The uncanny silence became oppressive as the perplexed worshippers fixed their gaze on their motionless Rebbe. After a very long pause, he finally explained:

> 'There, near the door, sits a Jew who all his life lived among non-Jews. And he cannot read Hebrew. When he saw the whole congregation standing in prayer, he was seized by a feeling of envy. He began to cry and sobbingly said: 'Father in Heaven, You know all prayers, their source and meaning, and I only know a few letters of the alphabet. Here, I offer you *aleph, beth, gimmel, daled* (the first four letters of the Hebrew alphabet), and You, in Your great mercy, arrange these letters into prayers!' 'Now,' concluded the Rebbe, 'God is busy ordering the letters of that devout man; hence we must wait before we can blow the *Shofar*'.

In this story is reflected the religious tragedy of our times.

We have, in our synagogues, not just one solitary Jew who cannot read Hebrew properly and follow the congregation in prayer; we have many. But who cries? Who feels anguished and heart-broken because of his illiteracy? If Judaism were really as close to us as it should be, ought there not be rivers of tears flowing from the eyes of those who, perhaps through no fault of their own, cannot even read and understand the language of their people? Would we not expect our children to cry if, on occasionally visiting us, they could not speak and comprehend our language; should we not then weep grief-stricken when we are unable to read and understand God's word in the holy tongue of our Torah and Prophets?

This humble Jew in the story, who was overcome by shame and envy, certainly made sure that the following year he could join the congregation by learning some Hebrew in the meantime. If some of our congregants would have this feeling of inadequacy, they might well be able to follow our services next year; for they would feel the urge to overcome their handicap in the intervening months by studying Hebrew.

But this applies also to those who can read and understand their prayers. Are there any with lachrymose eyes at our services? Recall the fervour and feeling that welled within the hearts and eyes of our parents and grandparents when they cried before God 'May it be your will O God, Who hearkens to the voice of weeping, to store our tears in Your flask...'

Do our prayers really touch us, grip our heart, seize our soul, penetrate our innermost depths?

Our inability to cry in an outpouring of prayer is symptomatic of the shallowness of present-day religion. The stream of religion today, as has often been said, is one mile wide and one inch deep. Our religious devotion is external, formal, conventional, even fashionable, but it has not conquered our heart and mind. Yes, we go along with religious practices and other good deeds, but often our heart is not fully with us. The *Weltschmerz* does not touch us sufficiently. When we see a Jew violating the Sabbath, or hear of one guilty of unethical or immoral conduct, does our heart really bleed as if pierced by a dagger? When we see a poor man and cannot help him, do we inwardly weep with compassion? When Yeshivoth or synagogues or other vital institutions struggle under the burden of debts inhibiting their progress, how many of us are really distressed and bothered to the point of torment, as we would be for lack of means to feed our own children?

These failings are all manifestations of a religion that leaves us cold and without passion. This religion without tears may explain the paradox of our present condition: While the religious revolution has moved forward in giant strides, morality has declined. To this baffling problem we will turn our attention next time.

As we now plead, then, for the blessings of life and health and peace, let us remember the saying in the Talmud: '**From the day the Temple was destroyed, the gates of prayer were shut; yet the gates of tears were never closed**.'[53]

In this spirit let us pray with redoubled fervour and earnestness: *ya'aleh kolenu me'erev, veyavo tzidkenu miboker, veyera'eh pidyonenu ad erev,* 'May our voice ascend this evening, leading to our righteous conduct in the morning, so that our redemption may appear as night concludes this holy day.'

3. The Burdens of the Rabbi's Labour*

If there is a divine service that is unique, it is certainly *Kol Nidrei*. It is the only time when we wear a *Tallith* at night. The *Kil Nidrei* prayer itself is without parallel in our liturgy. And the solemnity of our melodies and atmosphere tonight make this service altogether incomparable among the year's religious experiences.

It is also distinguished for one less obvious feature contributing to its uniqueness: It is the only service of the year at which the rabbi serves in a specifically rabbinical capacity.

---

*The third of five addresses delivered at the Fifth Avenue Synagogue, New York, during the High Holydays, 5725–1964.

We open the service with a declaration by the rabbi, joined by two other elders, formally constituting a rabbinical court: *Biyeshivah shel ma'alah uviyeshivah shel mattah...anu matirin lehithpalel im ha'avaryonim.* 'At the session of the Heavenly court above, and at the session of the earthly court below...we grant permission to pray with the sinners.'

This probably is a flashback to the time of the Marranos, or crypto-Jews, who during the Spanish Inquisition had outwardly surrendered their Jewish faith to preserve their lives, but who wished to rejoin their brethren on Yom Kippur to demonstrate their secret attachment to Judaism. Since they had undergone conversion to another faith, their admission required the formal sanction of an ecclesiastical court.

In contrast, then, to all other services of the year, when the rabbi is essentially an ordinary worshipper like anybody else and without any distinctly rabbinical functions, tonight is the only occasion in our synagogue ritual when the rabbi exercises a rabbinical prerogative, at least nominally.

This may be a suitable occasion, therefore, to depart from the usual practice and devote our reflections on *Kol Nidrei* night not to the ideals, duties and shortcomings of the congregation, but to speak instead of the rabbi's ideals, duties and shortcomings. Tonight I shall tell you of the rabbi's labours, lead you into the inner sanctum of the rabbi's conscience and work-motives, his stresses, despairs and rewards, his frustrations and compensation.

The Talmud tells of a Sage who, on ordaining two young rabbis, sounded this note of caution: 'Do you really think that I give you dominion over others? No, servitude I give you.'[54]

Never was this more true than today, when spiritual leadership is confronted with unprecedented challenges and opposition.

More than ever before, countless rabbis are subjected to cruel anti-religious pressures, to organized attempts battering their conscience into submission to breaches of their faith and convictions. The past year in particular has witnessed ugly and widely broadcast efforts to coerce the conscience of some of the world's leading rabbis, including the Chief Rabbis of Israel and of England, to modify religious rulings they issued under vicious pressures of government and press campaigns.

This night, then, is an opportune time for an appraisal of the functions and burdens of the rabbinate.

The modern rabbi in Western lands is indeed a far cry from his classic counterpart of the past.

He is charged with the conduct of services. He has to be an organizer, administrator, fund-raiser, after-dinner speaker, marriage counsellor, sick visitor, funeral official, all in one. Often, especially in America, he functions also as a news commentator, political analyst, book reviewer, film critic, freedom rider, ghost writer – and sometimes, amidst all other tasks, as a spiritual leader and teacher.

Formerly, the rabbi was, as the Hebrew term *rabbi* implies, principally a teacher, a judge, an authority on Jewish law. His main preoccupation was to *pasken sha'aloth,* to give religious rulings on questions submitted to him and educate people to ask such questions.

The difference is perhaps best illustrated by the varied usages of the rabbi's place of activity. To describe his area of jurisdiction, and competence, one used to speak of a rabbi's *kiseh harabbanuth*, a 'throne' or 'seat of the rabbinate.' He ruled, he *sat* and learned. Now we speak of a rabbi's pulpit – he *stands* and talks.

There is a story of one congregation's officers who engaged a new rabbi. When he stipulated that he wanted enough time and opportunity to learn for a couple of hours every day, they told him: 'We don't want a rabbi who still has to learn; we want a rabbi who has his studies behind him and who knows.'

With all the multifarious duties and activities of the modern rabbi, one is reminded of the legend about the great and saintly Rabbi Levi Yitzchak. When he was about to be born, Satan complained that if that great soul were to descend on earth, it would reform the world, and his own power would come to an end. But the Holy One, blessed be He, comforted Satan, and said: 'But he will be a rabbi, and he will be too occupied with communal affairs.'

Complaints *against* rabbis, sometimes spiced with pungent cynicism, are not new. Over 150 years ago the outstanding Chasidic master, Rabbi Nachman of Bratzlav, berated the rabbis of his time with biting wit, saying: 'It was hard for Satan alone to mislead the whole world, so he appointed prominent rabbis in different localities.'

But much older and more persistent are complaints *by* rabbis against those in their charge.

The very first rabbi in history, *Mosheh rabbenu,* Moses our Rabbi or Teacher, already cried out in despair: *Eichah essa levadi torchachem umasachem verivchem,* 'How can I bear by myself your troubles and your burdens and your strife.'[55] *Eicha essa levadi,* 'How can I bear by myself,' alone. What oppressed Moses about carrying out the burdens of his office was above all his loneliness. A true rabbi often suffers terrible loneliness.

These days we frequently hear of the loneliness of an American President in his awesome office. But his is neither a social nor an intellectual isolation. He can freely share with his friends their ideals and their pastimes – even their jokes. He can dance with other people's wives, let alone with his own, he can eat at any of their homes, and he can even make a little fortune on the side like anyone else. He is lonely only when he makes decisions of state, and then for no more than eight years; otherwise he lives completely in the world of his friends.

Not so the rabbi. Though he attends more wedding parties and crowded dinners than most people, he is often very lonely indeed. Having to practice what he preaches, and preaching much that is unpopular, he lives a life apart. To him many of the pleasures and concerns of his closest friends are out of bounds. He must be above politics and beyond the temptation of business speculation. In fact, he often lives in a different world from those surrounding him.

His worries are scarcely theirs – how to influence people and make friends for Yeshivoth or *Mikvoth,* or how to unravel a knotty halachic problem. His thrills are not always theirs – such as when he has succeeded in winning a Jew for Sabbath observance or for attendance at daily services in the synagogue. His scale of values in rating and respecting people has to be different. To him, a humble, kindly, pious person tucked away on some backseat may be a really great and distinguished man compared to some big name whom everybody honours although his possessions hardly include rectitude, piety or scholarship.

The rabbi even judges his own sermons differently. When his congregants look for a message that is timely, up-to-date like the latest newspaper, he may search for what is timeless, imperishable like the Bible, as topical today as it was centuries ago and as it will be for all future times because it expresses eternal verities. When his listeners react: 'I enjoyed your sermon,' he may prefer them to say: 'I cannot say that I enjoyed your sermon; but you have convinced me that your plea is right, and I will try to change my ways accordingly.'

The rabbi is lonely in his working hours when he broods over a sermon. He is lonely in his leisure hours when he studies. Sometimes he is even lonely when he prays in the synagogue while others talk or idle, or when he conducts a class and only a handful of people attend.

Innumerable are the occasions when he exclaims with Moses: *Eichah essa levadi*, 'How can I bear alone...'

Moses then referred specifically to three anxieties that beset him: *torchachem umasachem verivchem*, 'Your troubles and your burdens and your strife.'

According to Nachmanides, *torchachem*, 'your troubles,' refers to the trouble Moses experienced in teaching the laws of the Torah to Israel. The rabbi's foremost effort must be to teach, to instruct.

How difficult it is to teach laws regarded by so many as obsolete or too hard; to preach that man's aim should be not to have a good time but to make the times good! How much trouble one encounters to explaining the primacy of the spirit in an age of materialism, the joys of goodness and decency in an era of cheap pleasures, the virtue of humility and self-sacrifice in times of self-advertisement and material ambition! How much hardship a rabbi invites by constantly swimming against the stream, by advocating a religious discipline which demands daily expenses and restraints, by setting a premium on feelings of guilt and a penalty on a life of ease. 'How can I bear your trouble...'

Umasachem, 'your burdens,' is a reference to Moses's prayer for the community. The rabbi's second chief task is to plead and intercede for his congregation and its members.

His greatest 'burden' is to feel the sufferings of the poor, experience the grief of the bereaved and the anguish of the sick, to have the fullest of empathy that parents possess for their young, to cry out to God for the welfare and health of his flock as he would for his own children. He has to pray hard, for he knows that he will be held to account for the failings of his congregation. As its leader he is responsible for the religious education and conduct of each individual in his charge. 'How can I bear your burden...'

Lastly, concludes Nachmanides, *verivchem,* 'your strife', refers to the duties of Moses as a judge in litigations and disputes. This represents the third of the rabbi's main tasks.

It is the rabbi's function to make peace where there is argument or strife, to reconcile enemies, to dispense justice in quarrels brought before him for arbitration. This, too, is hard. How embarrassing it often is to tell a person, 'You are wrong, or selfish,' 'you must apologize, or pay compensation.' Nothing is more thankless than to be a judge over other people's conduct. Yet that is the task of the rabbi, and he cannot evade it. In fact, Jewish law insists that disputes among Jews must not be brought before non-Jewish courts; they should be referred to a rabbi or a *Beth Din,* a rabbinical court, for settlement at a *Din Torah,* a religious arbitration in accordance with our own rules of justice and equity. Not so long ago such *Batei Din* existed in every Jewish community, and the discharge of this responsibility belonged to the rabbi's most exacting preoccupations however difficult and often unpleasant an assignment it was. 'How can I bear your strife...'

We acclaim God every day in the *Shemoneh Esreh* as *rofeh ne'eman verachaman,* 'a faithful and merciful Healer.' This contrasts with a human doctor who heals either with *emunah,* with 'faith,' or with *rachmanuth,* with 'compassion.' If he is faithful, he cannot be guided by pity; he must be firm and sometimes even cruel. He may have to sink a knife into the tender flesh of his patient, he has to jab needles, prescribe bitter pills, and insist on rest and diet without mercy. And if he is *rachaman*, 'compassionate,' he cannot be *ne'eman*, 'faithful', to the dictates of medicine. He must make his choice, for only God is a Healer who can be *ne'eman* and *rachaman* at the same time.

Similarly the rabbi, the human healer of souls. He too must often choose being either *ne'eman* or *rachaman*, between giving people what they need or what they want. If he is faithful, he must be firm and sometimes harsh. He must prescribe strict rest on Sabbaths and a rigid diet of *Kashruth* every day. He may be called upon to break up the love between a Jewish boy and his non-Jewish girlfriend, or to reprove his own friend for moral or religious lapses without pity. And if he is soft, guided only by 'humanitarian' feelings, or by the desire to please and flatter, he cannot be faithful to the dictates of Judaism. If he preaches a religion of comfort, a Judaism without tears and hardship, without discipline and restraints, he betrays his faith and abdicates his function. Only God can combine *ne'eman* and *rachaman; midath hadin*, 'the rule of justice', with *midath harachamim*, 'the rule of mercy.' But human judges are commanded: *Ani verosh hatzdiku*, 'do justice to the afflicted and the destitute,'[56] on which the Midrash comments: *Terachemu eino omer, elah hatzdiku*, 'It does not say "have mercy" but "do justice".'[57]

Of course, many rabbis, even the best and most sincere among them, are often tempted, like Jonah, to take the line of least resistance and flee from their divine calling. Frustrated and discouraged, they choose to escape because they cannot bear up under the load – to proclaim unpleasant truths to unwilling listeners, threaten punishment to those who rebel against

God or resort to unethical practices against their fellow men. How can a rabbi be frank with a solitary patient whose pains become acute as he lies in bed and he feels puzzled and cruelly abandoned to his fate? Would it answer his questions on why he suffered if he were told that perhaps he had defied God's law and desecrated the Sabbath? Frankness would require the rabbi to pursue his mission with a touching faith. How could he sit calmly by when spouses seek to consult him on their unhappy marriages? How could he venture a judgment that perhaps they had failed to uphold the Jewish family laws which are calculated to ennoble husband–wife relations? What explanations could a rabbi offer to parents whose sons turned against them by marrying out of the faith? How could he summon the courage to tell them that maybe the fault was theirs, having failed to instil Jewish loyalties in their child? Perhaps they had cared more for giving him music and dancing instructions than Hebrew lessons in his childhood and adolescence. How could a rabbi encourage people to be severe in judging their own faults and failings, and be charitable in criticizing others or complaining against God?

These are all challenges to daunt the stoutest heart, assignments to make even a prophet flee and a Moses exclaim: 'How can I bear…'

But for all these burdens and frustrations there are also great compensations.

Greater even than the joy of a doctor who has helped to restore his patient to life or health is the joy of a rabbi who has succeeded in bringing some comfort to a broken heart, in inducing a smile on a face worn with cares and worry, in opening the eyes of a worshipper to the splendour of our faith, and restoring a distraught soul to religious life and spiritual health.

Greater than the thrill of a politician who wins an election landslide is the delight of a rabbi who wins a congregation to religious fervour and piety.

Greater than the elation of a captain of industry who has brought off a big and profitable deal is the elation of a rabbi who has prevailed on a member to invest his profits in the service of Jewish education or charity.

And greater than the satisfaction of a lawyer who has won a case in court is the satisfaction of a rabbi who has won a case for God and goodness in an argument with a perplexed soul.

A rabbi never labours in vain, so long as he preaches and practices the word of God. In the lovely analogy of the Prophet Isaiah:

> Just as the rain cometh down and the snow from Heaven, and returneth not thither, except it water the earth and make it bring forth and bud, giving seed to the sower and bread to the eater, so shall My word be that goeth forth out of My mouth; it shall not return unto Me empty, except it accomplish that which I please and make the thing whereto I sent it prosper.[58]

No doctor or lawyer can ever share with all his patients or clients his professional interests and activities for a complete day, or indeed at any time. No man of any calling or profession can have the soul-stirring happiness experienced by a rabbi on Yom Kippur, when for a full day his world is completely identical with the world of those he serves. He has the high privilege to guide an entire congregation in effecting atonement before God and reconciliation among men. He can operate on a hundred hearts without shedding blood and inspire countless homes without passing their threshold. He is empowered to announce to his flock seeking repentance in truth on behalf of their Creator and Judge: *Salachti kidvarecha*, 'I have pardoned according to your request.'

יזכר

Yizkor

1. Reflections on the Jewish Concept of After-life*

> This world is like an ante-chamber before the world-to-come; prepare yourself in the ante-chamber so that you may enter the main hall![59]

The theme for our reflections this morning is certainly the most difficult religious subject of all. How can one explain our belief in the world-to-come, in after-life or the here-after, to modern-thinking people in our sophisticated age? Perhaps even the belief in God is a more rational concept and easier to accept than the belief in after-life, in the immortality of the soul. Surely this is purely a matter of faith. It cannot be discovered in test-tubes, proved by mathematical formulae or philosophical reasoning. There is no historical evidence for the existence of 'the next world'; no one has yet returned from heaven and told us what to anticipate there.

And if this is a matter of sheer faith or blind belief, why even try to explain it? Those who believe require no convincing, and those who do not, how can they be convinced?

The problem is not unlike that of mourners stunned and perplexed by a terrible bereavement. As the sainted Chofetz Chayim once put it, for those who have faith there are no questions, and for those who have no faith there are no answers.

---

*Sermon preached before *Yizkor* on Yom Kippur 5723–1962, at the Fifth Avenue Synagogue, New York.

Yet the belief in the here-after is undoubtedly one of the cardinal teachings of Judaism, enunciated as an integral part of our faith in the Talmud and by leading Jewish philosophers. It is implied in numerous biblical passages, such as when Balaam exclaimed: 'May I die the death of the righteous, and my latter end be like his;'[60] and when Abigail told David: 'and the soul of my master will be bound up in the bond of life (after his death).'[61] This phrase has become the key-note in our memorial prayer for the departed. The belief in a here-after is also taken for granted by the Preacher when he cries out '... And the dust returns to the earth as it was, but the spirit returns unto God who gave it,'[62] and in the elegiac prayer of the Psalmist: 'For You will not abandon my soul to Sheol.'[63]

This belief has been derided by the ancient pagans as well as by the modern sceptics. It is related of the Greek cynic philosopher Diogenes that he instructed his students to cast his body onto a field after his death. 'But ravens will consume your flesh,' declaimed his disciples. 'Then place a stick in my hand so that I can drive the ravens away,' he answered. When the disciples argued that one cannot move after death, Diogenes retorted: 'In that case what difference does it make, what do I care if the ravens eat my flesh?'

This is the same attitude that our moderns have adopted toward cremation after death. The same attitude prevails among those who advocate unlimited autopsies on the dead. For them death is the final end, denying as they do the belief in a here-after for body and soul.

I.

In my attempt to find some explanation for the here-after, I searched and found in a recent rabbinical work[64] an exposition which is simple and yet profound, rational and at the same time poetic in its beauty and power.

Imagine an unborn child in the mother's womb who is endowed with a fully developed mind and senses. As it lies there crouching its head between the knees and feeding on the mother's sustenance, it would doubtless regard its dark, confined space within the mother as its entire world and the period of its foetal growth as its span of life.

Now imagine there were twins, who were speculating on their fate to be. 'What is to become of us after we leave the womb and depart from our universe?'

From what they see and feel around them, they could not possibly have the slightest notion of life after their separation from the mother.

Now imagine one twin has faith and claims some knowledge of a future life after leaving the mother, while the other is a sceptic, believing only what his senses and mind can perceive – only in 'this world.'

The first argues: 'I have faith – sustained by a long tradition passed on to me – that on leaving the womb, we will enter a new life of much broader dimensions.' And he tells what tradition has taught him; that on their departure, they would eat by mouth, see with their eyes, stretch out their legs and walk on the face of a vast earth, which features seas and mountains, plants and beautiful skies above.

But the other twin scoffs at this 'simpleton.' 'Only a fool can believe all these fairy tales which the mind cannot grasp.' 'And according to you', asks the child of faith, 'what will happen to us after we depart from the womb?' 'That is simple', answers the 'enlightened' sceptic. 'When we depart from this world of ours, our food supply will cut off and we will drop into the abyss from which there is no return.'

As they talked, the womb opened. The 'simpleton' departs first. The 'rational' twin, still inside, trembles with shock and grief at the 'misfortune' that befell his brother. He cries and mourns: 'Brother, where are you? Woe is me for your destruction!' As he bewails the loss of his brother, he hears a terrible shriek from his fellow-twin just outside the womb. The brother inside shakes with terror and exclaims: 'Woe, this is his final agonizing death-cry as his life is snuffed out.'

While this yet-unborn twin grieves and wails over his brother's 'death,' there is rejoicing and festivity in the home of the new-born. The parents and relatives celebrate and greet each other: *'Mazal Tov, Mazal Tov* **– a son is born to us!'**

What a powerful illustration, this, on one hand, for our inability to grasp life beyond this finite world and, on the other hand, for the infinite life in store for us. If there is such a difference between the world of the womb and our universe, how much vaster must the difference be between our physical world and the spiritual life the soul enters on leaving the confinement of the body!

Just as the 'enlightened' brother who remained in the womb could not visualize that the brother who departed from the mother did not die but, on the contrary, ventured forth into a wide world from a miniature one, so can the wisest man on earth, applying pure reason, have no conception of the soul's life after it is freed and delivered from the body at a new birth. Anyone who therefore mocks at the idea of a here-after, who maintains that the death of the body is the end, and that nothing more vast, more perfect and infinite awaits him, is like the cocksure and defiant twin inside the womb who mourned the departure of his brother from his world.

The exit from the womb is the birth of the body; and the exit from the body is the real birth of the soul. Hence the Preacher's statement, 'Better...is the day of death than the day of one's birth.'[65] This gives a rather different twist to Mark Twain's witticism: 'Why is it that we rejoice at a birth and grieve at a funeral? It is because we are not the persons involved.'

II.

Let us now venture one step further in our exploration, not of outer space but of what is beyond it. What kind of future existence does Jewish tradition hold forth for us? What joys await us that moved our Sages to say: 'Better one hour of blissfulness in the world-to-come then all the life in this world'?[66]

Maimonides[67] illumines our understanding of this abstract subject with a penetrating analogy. The blind cannot visualize colours and the deaf cannot imagine music, just as a fish cannot have any concept of fire. Hence (elaborating the thought of Maimonides), the joy of a connoisseur in beholding a beautiful painting of a great master can never be experienced by the blind, and the thrill of a music-lover listening to a wonderful symphony is inaccessible to the deaf.

Now, in this world our common joys are mainly physical: delectable food, elegant clothes, material success, marital delights, and the like. All these joys are non-existent in the world-to-come which has only purely spiritual joys to offer. As the Talmud asserts: 'In the world-to-come there is no eating, no drinking, no trading, no sensual pleasures; but the righteous sit, with their crowns adorning their heads, and enjoy the splendour of the Divine Presence.'[68] The only pleasures available, then, are the infinite joy of perceiving the majesty of the Divine truth, justice, mercy and harmony – the beholding of the ultimate perfection. But these pleasures can be enjoyed only by those who have trained themselves in this world to appreciate such joys, to be sensitive to purely spiritual delights. To develop such sensibility requires constant intellectual and spiritual exercises on earth; it comes to those who in their lifetime have learned the supreme fascination of religious studies, the thrill of witnessing the triumph of right over might, the utter joy of bringing succour to the weak and the needy, the perfect contentment springing from faith and hope, and the happy ecstasy of contemplating the attributes and wondrous works of the Creator.

Think of visitors to an art gallery or a concert hall. Those who have cultivated an appreciation of the arts through years of study and artistic pursuits will derive the fullest enjoyment from what they see or hear, whilst those who never indulged in such pursuits but limited their interests to idle or mundane pleasures will feel bored and lonely. So also in the world-to-come where our spiritual self will be what we have made of it while on earth. The spiritually cultured souls will reap the reward of susceptivity to the entrancement with the Divine glory around them, whilst the others will be condemned to unmitigated boredom, loneliness and disgrace for all eternity.

Yom Kippur gives us a foretaste of these purely spiritual joys in store for us. On this day we are close to the sublime state of angels. We mortify our flesh by denying ourselves our common physical pleasures. As in the world-to-come, there is today no eating, no drinking, no trading, no marital relations. The sole fascination offered by this Holy Day lies in our extraordinary religious experience, our immersion into the world of prayer and godliness, our thrill at ridding ourselves from our feelings of guilt, and our contentment at being at peace with ourselves, our neighbours and our God.

III.

There is of course also another form of immortality, one which is perhaps more easily understood than the spiritual existence in the here-after of which we have been speaking until now.

It is this second expression of immortality on which we are to reflect now, as we are about to remember those dear ones who, released from the confinement of this *alma dishikra*, 'world of falsehood,' have been born into the eternity of the *olam ha'emeth*, 'the world of truth,' in the language of our rabbis.

Literally, it lies in our power to make our parents and ancestors immortal. 'Whenever I have to make an important decision in life, I ask myself: "what would my sainted father אז״ל counsel me to do in this situation, how would he want me to act?" And so my father, though long departed, still lives and guides me just as he did when he was still among the living.' By setting up our deceased parents and forebears as our constant mentors and advisors, by acting always in harmony with their way of life and wishes, we not only preserve their spirit alive, but we make them instruct and lead us from the grave as they did while on earth. They are thus no more dead than is the influence they continue to exert on us.

In this sense we also have it within our power to make *ourselves* immortal. To this day in countless Jewish homes and houses of learning one can hear such phrases as 'Rashi says,' 'the Rambam rules,' or 'the *Chofetz Chayim* holds.' These creative giants of the spirit still talk to us, still govern our conduct, though they left this earth long ago. The work of their lives has never ceased. They are all immortal. Likewise our life will be great and imperishable to the extent that our wisdom will inspire men, our munificence will help the poor and the sick, our vision will enlighten our successors, even after we have departed from this world.

Some of us may still exercise an influence 25 years after our departure, perhaps through a hospital we helped build to heal sick bodies, or a synagogue we helped erect to repair sick souls. The great among us may still be active among the living 50 years after death, perhaps through a book we wrote or children we helped to educate. The greatest in our midst may radiate their brilliance hundreds of years beyond their passing, maybe by creating a powerful movement to affect the course of history or by composing a classic work of art or literature.

But all of us, whether endowed with exceptional talents or not, the humblest as well as the mightiest, can – if we but want – become immortal and leave an indelible mark on history through the contribution of our means and energies, whether great or small, towards ridding the world of evil, substituting virtue for vice, and our indispensable share in speeding the day when the Kingdom of God will be brought down from the next world to the reality of this world when the Prophetic vision will be realized: '**He will destroy death forever; and the Lord God will wipe away tears from off all faces, and the reproach of His people shall He remove from all the earth**.'[69]

2. 'With All Thy Might' – Ethics and Religion

> Is such the fast that I have chosen, the day for a man to afflict himself, is he to bow down his head like a bulrush, and to spread sackcloth and ashes under him? Is not this the fast that I have chosen:
>
> To loose the fetters of wickedness, to undo the bands of the yoke, and to let the oppressed go free, and that you break every yoke? Is it not to deal your bread to the hungry, and that you bring the poor that are cast out to your house;
>
> When you see the naked, that you cover him, and that you hide not yourself from your own flesh?[70]

Nowhere in the vast storehouse of the world's literature, religious or secular, is there a nobler definition of man's duty to man than in these exquisite lines from this morning's Haphtorah. What a superb introduction this is to the third fundamental requisite for 'averting the evil decree' – *tsedakah*, 'righteousness' and to the third faculty with which we are to love God: *bechol me'odecha*, 'with all your means.'

Repentance and prayer are the indispensable foundations of Judaism. But without *tsedakah*, righteous conduct, these virtues are like a strong substructure sunk into the ground with nothing built on it. Our fasting, our religious exercises, our reconciliation with God are meaningless, unless they lead to righteous deeds.

What then is *tsedakah*? This unique Hebrew word has two meanings: Righteousness in the widest sense, and charity in the narrower sense. These two meanings are distinctly mentioned by the Prophet – '…To loose the fetters of wickedness …' and 'to deal your bread to the hungry…'

These two meanings correspond to the two major symbols of Yom Kippur: Fasting and white clothes.

'The reward of fasting is charity,' says the Talmud.[71] The fast makes us feel the pangs of hunger. It makes us experience the distress of want. For once we share the pain of hunger with the poor. If tonight with the conclusion of our fast we should fail to think of those who suffer hunger because they have nothing to eat, we would have been merciless beyond words. For nothing can excuse or mitigate the cruelty of him who, having experienced what it is like to go without food for one day, does not care to help those who have to go without adequate food every day. Hence the Talmud adds 'Anyone who defers the distribution of charity overnight following any fast day is as if he was shedding blood.'[72] That is the plain message of Yom Kippur on the subject of simple charity.

The white clothes we wear on Yom Kippur, as the High Priest did when he made atonement for the people in the Holy of Holies, consist of the *Kittel*, the garment that will one day serve as *Tachrichim*, the shrouds accompanying us in the grave. Yom Kippur is to remind us of the time when we shall all have to accept what Judaism regards as the noblest form of charity in the wide sense: *chesed shel emeth*, 'loving kindness of truth.'[73] For services to the dead are rendered without any self-interest. The dead cannot repay the kindness of the living. There can be no expectation of plaques or honours, or of services in return. Of such disinterested performance of 'righteousness' in its truest sense Yom Kippur is to remind us.

Why, you may ask, does the Jewish concept of ethics, of noble conduct, require any religious support and motivation? Why can we not espouse a secular morality, like scientific humanism or ethical culture? Why is Judaism so implacably opposed to divorcing *tsedakah* from *teshuvah* and *tefilah*; to isolating *gemilath chasadim*, the practice of good deeds, from *torah* and *avodah*, from religious learning and worship? Can there be no goodness without God? Do we not all know many people, Jews and Gentiles, who have warm hearts and noble souls, who liberally support good causes and who are upright in all their dealings, without worshipping God formally or even acknowledging Him?

There are three principal answers to these questions:

Firstly, absolute standards of ethics cannot exist without God. The ancient Greeks believed that it was right to expose crippled children to die in the woods so that they would not be a burden to society. To the Eskimos it is a virtue for children to kill their own parents when they become too old to maintain themselves. Many Nazis were no doubt sincerely convinced, in all conscience, that they were rendering a meritorious service to mankind by wiping out Jews and gypsies as 'sub-human races' plaguing society. The communists treasure the interest of the state more than individual freedom.

Our sense of justice condemns all these attitudes as diabolically evil. But if we affirm that good and evil are values to be determined by the arbitrary whims of one's conscience, by what right can we condemn the ethical aberrations of the Greeks or Eskimos? On what basis can we brand as immoral the murderous practices of the Nazis and communists? Perhaps they are right and we are wrong. Have they not as much right to determine what is ethical as we do?

Human consciences are as capricious as they are diverse. What appears ethical to one may be immoral to another. The recent controversy over the Newburgh welfare code is a striking example of how human opinions based on mere conscience can divide on matters of right and wrong.

Judaism insists, therefore, that there must be a Higher Authority than man's fickle conscience to define what is ethical, that the absolute standards of right and good can be determined only in relation to the revealed will of God.

Secondly, secular ethics is inferior in quality to religious ethics.

Many great philanthropists will gladly write out cheques for deserving causes; yet should some wretched beggar or *Meschulach* knock at the door of their home or office, he will be told by the maid or secretary that they are not in. Charitable people who fear God do not behave that way.

There are businessmen who enjoy the highest reputation for integrity and yet will have no qualms to treat their employees with exacting harshness, address them crudely and hurt their feelings. Truly religious persons do not behave in this manner. They know that all humans are brothers, equally created in the image of God, and they will treat the lowliest subordinate, the most menial servant, with the same kindness and consideration as they treat a millionaire friend.

How often does one hear otherwise fine and decent men say: 'I am a good Jew', or 'I give so much charity.' This too is a flaw in a man's ethical make-up. Deeply devout people never indulge in self-praise. A refined sense of humility is their hallmark. When ethics is combined with religious faith, pride gives way to modesty, and self-esteem surrenders to self-criticism in the constant search for higher ideals.

Thirdly, and most important, secular ethics is degrading; it robs life of a supreme goal and purpose. By making success instead of service the highest aim in life, we often confuse means with ends. Life itself is subordinated to the enterprises necessary for making a living.

A well-known writer has with justice asked: 'It is not possible that man will learn to conduct business without being dominated by Business? May not the future leadership in business undertakings belong to those whose vision is not limited to business success?'[74]

That surely is the deeper meaning of the witty remark made by a great eighteenth-century rabbi: '**Some people think of business when they are in the synagogue; is it too much to ask them to think of God when they are at business**?'[75]

In the Jewish view, integrity of character is an integral part of religious piety. The practice of ethics is ennobling only if it belongs to our worship of God. For *tsedakah* implies that the motive for all our endeavours, whether occupational or charitable, is the urge within us to serve and help each other. True, *tsedakah* calls on me to rejoice in my neighbour's success as much as in my own, for we are both engaged in promoting the common good in compliance with God's will.

We are about to intone the *Yizkor* Service. In that hallowed memorial prayer for the departed souls we make a peculiarly worded pledge. The text reads: *Yizkor Elokim eth nishmath avi mori…shehalach le'olamo ba'avur she'ani noder tsedakah ba'ado…*, 'May God remember the soul of my revered father…who has passed on to his world, *by virtue of my pledge to give charity for his sake…*'

What is this, a commercial transaction? Does God need our reminder to remember?

No, God's remembrance requires neither a cue nor payment. Charity is meant to bring God to us. As the Talmud puts it: 'He that gives a penny to the poor merits to greet the Divine Presence, as is written: "As for me, I shall behold Your Presence in righteousness (or through charity)".'[76]

Every time we perform a good or charitable deed on earth God remembers our parents who gave birth to us and trained us to do good. By reciting *Yizkor* (lit. 'He *will* remember') after making a pledge to donate charity we merely *state* that our act of kindness will redound to the credit of our father and mother in the eyes of God.

As we remember, then, our beloved kinsfolk, we are to rededicate ourselves to a life of righteousness, consecrated by religious faith, which is grounded in the Prophet's sublime promise in our *Haphtorah*: 'Then shall your light break forth as the morning, and your healing shall spring forth speedily; and your *righteousness shall go before you*, the glory of the Lord shall be your reward. Then shall you call, and the Lord will answer; you shall cry, and He will say: "Here I am".'[77]

3. The Moral Revolution

Among the most striking features of the entire Yom Kippur services is the choice of our biblical readings for the day. Out of the four – two from the Torah and two from the Prophets – three do not mention Yom Kippur at all. Only this morning's Torah reading actually referred to the Day of Atonement, setting forth the ritual in the ancient Temple. The other three readings from Scriptures focus attention on a different subject altogether.

Our *Haphtorah* of this morning gave us Isaiah's stirring plea for righteousness. The fast God delights in, he proclaims in this majestic message, is not just our abstention from eating and drinking, wearing sackcloth and ashes, or indulging in religious rites; it is rather the abstention from fraud and oppression, depriving ourselves of bread to give to the hungry, opening our homes to the poor and clothing the naked.

For *Minchah* this afternoon our Torah reading concerns forbidden marriages and the rules of sexual morality, whilst the *Haphtorah* relates the story of Jonah, the most dramatic story ever told of a city condemned to destruction because of immoral and unethical practices and eventually saved from its doom by repentance.

The religious inspiration of Yom Kippur, then, like Judaism itself, wants to make of us not only better Jews in the narrow ritual sense, but also better human beings. The biblical messages of Yom Kippur are primarily concerned with moral failings – not just our own but also those of the non-Jewish world, as exemplified by the story of Jonah's mission to pagan Niniveh.

Clearly, then, in selecting the most significant passages from the Bible for reading on this supremely holy day, our Sages placed the main emphasis on our moral regeneration.

All the revolutions we discussed so far on these Days of Awe have propelled man forward with a mighty thrust. The freedom movements have brought independence to more nations and the hope of equal treatment to more individuals in a single decade than a millennium in the past. The scientific revolution has suddenly rocketed us forward to the most thrilling adventures in outer space and into the mysteries of the tiny atom, adding more to our knowledge of nature in 20 years than had previously been accumulated since the beginning of time. The religious revolution has transformed bigotry into understanding, and given religion an uplift, status and respectability it has not enjoyed in a hundred years.

But morally, we seem to be slipping back into the barbarism of antiquity, to the garish ostentation of ancient Rome, to the body-worshipping cult of the Greeks, to the obscene perversities of the pagans, and to the shameless immodesty of the primitive jungle.

Applying the Isaiah passage from our *Haphtorah* to our times, we might well say that, instead of abstaining from fraud and oppression, we have turned crime into our major entertainment on the screen and in the news; instead of depriving ourselves of bread to give to the hungry, we deprive ourselves of bread to slim, and we waste our grain in giant silos when millions starve in the world; instead of opening our homes to strangers, we are often strangers in our own homes, having our good time elsewhere; and instead of clothing the naked, we display nudity and semi-nudity on beaches, in magazines, and sometimes even in more familiar places.

These charges require no substantiation for readers of our daily newspapers and weekly magazines. Every issue now features sickening stories of low life in high places, graft in government, fraud in big business, shameful divorces among popular celebrities, sordid murders in fashionable apartments, and a staggering increase in crime, vice, juvenile delinquency and dope addiction.

Perhaps you will say: 'Only the exceptions reach the newspaper columns, like air-crashes.'

But, if over one marriage in every four ends in divorce, that is no exception. If 13,000,000 American children today come from broken homes, that is no exception. If 85 per cent of all marriages among college students involve pre-marital pregnancies, that surely is no exception. And if two billion dollars are lost annually through employee thefts of money and merchandise, and if the United States is short each year of five billion dollars by income tax cheating, and if another two billion dollars are contributed annually to the new Temples of Paganism called funeral parlours, then we might with justice state that our moral order has, by and large, collapsed.

Now, you may ask, what is *our* role in this melancholy, revolting picture? And to the extent we are not personally involved, what is there that we can do to help clean the very air we breathe from its smutty pollen?

Everyone wears an air of self-righteousness. Drawing a blind over one's own affairs, one loves to gossip about the scandals of others.

Gossip itself is one of the greatest evils. Trading in scandal makes scandal a marketable commodity, and where there are sellers there are buyers.

Nothing so horrified our ancient rabbis as evil gossip. It ranked, in the language of the Talmud, as worse than bloodshed, idolatry or even incest.[78] For an evil tongue helps to circulate the poison of wrongdoing in the bloodstream of society, killing its entire organism. Hence our rabbis constantly warned us: '**Beware, shut your lips tight to evil speech, and close your ears to those assaulting you with it**!'

Shunning gossip like the plague is only one of the virtues stressed by Judaism in its unrelenting fight against evil, though this virtue is little respected or mentioned today.

Another value in Judaism is modesty or bashfulness. When Jeremiah castigated his contemporaries for their moral lapses and excesses, he listed their evil deeds and lashed out at the great and small alike: 'For from the least of them even unto the greatest of them, everyone is greedy for gain; and from the prophet even unto the priest, everyone dealeth falsely.'[79] His denunciation reached its climax of fury in the words: 'They are not even at all ashamed; neither know they even how to blush.'[80]

Just as religion requires tears to flourish, so does morality require the capacity to blush. But we blush with shame in the face of evil no more than we weep from the heart's depths in prayer.

How much less immorality would there be today if, instead of unashamedly looking at indecent figures or pictures, we would turn our eyes away in disgust. What woman would dare to profane the House of God by immodest attire, disporting herself as she might in an opera house or dance hall, if she knew her fellow-congregants would sink their blushing faces in shame at the sight of her? What Jew would publicly violate the Sabbath in front of any traditional synagogue by smoking or using a car, if he sensed that his brethren would be outraged and disgraced by his profanity? Who would dream of besmirching the innocence of youth with early dating, of soiling the purity of adolesence with pre-marital adventures, of demolishing the sanctity of marriage by adultery, or of debasing the glory of old age by salacious pleasures, if our society still had the horror born of shame for these evils, a horror which our forefathers cultivated so carefully?

Tz'ni-uth or bashfulness, an inborn shyness or reserve, used to be the hallmark of Jewish refinement. A sense of shame is one of the characteristics by which, according to Jewish law, one can determine whether a person belongs to the seed of Abraham.[81] Jews often have been guilty of many petty offenses, but immorality was as rare as was murder among them.

Today, we wantonly expunge these noble traits from our hearts and the hearts of our children. Parents are impatient if their sons and daughters have not begun to learn the art of courting and consorting at an age when their courts should still be schools and their consorts books. But these same parents are shocked and shattered if, after driving their children to be premature adults, they later behave as adults with the irresponsibility of children, getting involved in mischief and unhappy marriages.

Perhaps the worst of all the allies of evil is the connivance with it by silence. The silence of the Germans and the nations was the great scourge which sent six million Jews to the gas-chambers, and silence is the fertilizer which helps the weeds of evil to grow today.

One of the principal precepts in the Torah's code of holiness commands us: 'Thou shalt surely rebuke thy neighbour, and not bear sin with him.'[82] It is our religious duty to denounce evil wherever we find it. When we see our fellow-man committing a wrong, we have no right to stand by idly in silence. By failing to protest, even if our protest will be unheeded, we become accomplices in crime.

The majority of people are still happily honest and decent. But by our acquiescence or passivity we encourage the growth of vice.

Recently the abomination of our current funeral practices, 'the American Way of Death,' was widely publicized – at last. Are we not all guilty in raising this grisly monster? When we are invited to participate in the pagan custom of viewing the dead, do we wince? When we are offered, instead of the traditional plain pine box costing a few dollars, an ornate casket costing hundreds or thousands, with all the blood-curdling trimmings of embalming, dressing and other benefits, do we argue? When this death-tax helps to pour fortunes into private pockets instead of filling the coffers of the community for education and social service, as it ought to do and as it always did in Jewish communities in the past, do we cry out with indignation?

If we ask, then, how is it that we witness today at the same time a low ebb of morality and a rising tide of religion, there is but one answer: Where religion is not shallow and superficial but really taken seriously, moral standards are in fact secure. Among people who faithfully observe the Sabbath and *Kashruth,* who learn the Torah intensively and cherish its ideals, you will scarcely find illegitimate or delinquent children; in their homes you will see no obscene literature and hear no vulgar speech. Truly religious people do not gamble or defraud; they do not visit dens of vice, nor disport themselves indecently dressed.

The best proof for the moral effectiveness of a religious discipline can be found in Israel, where the geographical boundaries between religious and irreligious circles are often more clearly drawn than anywhere else. During my recent visit there I was told by a high government official that in the religious quarter of Mea Shearim, for instance, not a single case of juvenile delinquency had come to the notice of the police! In Beer Sheba a leading municipal official advised me that the social and moral difficulties widely encountered among Oriental children were incomparably reduced among the students of religious schools. The moral laxity and promiscuity so notorious in certain Kibbutzim simply do not exist in any religious Kibbutz.

Much of the blame for the moral decline of our times rests on our religious leadership, rabbis not excluded. We were meant to be the heirs of the Prophets: '**From the day the Temple was destroyed, prophecy was taken from the Prophets and given to the Sages, to rabbinical scholars**.'[83]

The Hebrew Prophets did not preach sermons in synagogues or temples. They went out to challenge evil where it was to be found. They assailed corrupt kings in their palaces, castigated the wicked in their dens, denounced greed and exploitation in the market place, and passionately cried out against immorality near the hiding-places of vice.

By confining our preachments to our sanctuaries, we preach largely to the converted. By limiting our public pronouncements to the banalities and platitudes acceptable to newspaper editors, we reduce the message of God to trite clichés and glib slogans.

Perhaps we ought to consider, following the Prophets' example, challenging corrupt politicians on their own platforms, attacking crooked business practices inside the citadels of commerce and finance, and proclaiming the wrath of God against the seducers of vice and immorality in marches on Hollywood, on night-clubs, music-halls, gambling dens and other cesspools of evil. We ought to cry out loud, likes Moses, until *Ha'azinu hashamayim vethishma ha'aretz*, 'the heavens will listen and the earth will hear.' By such dramatic demonstrations of God's ire, we may arouse the public conscience to feelings of shame and remorse, and to the danger of our civilization, like others before it, collapsing under the weight of its own moral turpitude.

We do not know how successful the Prophets were. Sometimes their warnings were heeded and the impending doom was averted, as in the story of Jonah who saved a mighty city by his effusion of God's anger.

On most occasions, their exhortations were spurned, and their prophecies of doom came to pass, as was the case with the destruction first of the Kingdom of Israel and then of the Kingdom of Judah.

The Prophets were lonely and unpopular people, hated by the men of power and wealth, ignored by the masses, and often persecuted by their temporal rulers.

But what difference does it make today whether they failed or succeeded at the time? The targets of their fury, the once mighty kings and princes, the iniquitous priests and exploiters, are dead and forgotten, while the Prophets, lonely and isolated at the time, are still immortal today and for all times. Their words are studied and proclaimed wherever we find civilized men, their ideals are to this day upheld as guideposts to perfection. Their message is not dimmed by the passage of time.

Is not the *Yizkor*-prayer our own effort to secure for our beloved kinsfolk a similar immortality beyond death? *Yizkor* means remembrance in the future. Is not everyone of us yearning, in the words of the Psalmist, 'that at his death he shall not take everything (down to the grave), that his glory shall not descend after him.'[84]

We can make ourselves and our forebears immortal, we can ensure '*Yizkor*,' that God and history 'will remember,' were we to aspire to be the Prophets of mankind and bring the ideal of Moses, the Father of Prophets, to realization: 'Would that all the people of the Lord were Prophets.'[85] For in the end, the truly immortal are only those who have had a share in bringing about the ultimate days when, in the glorious words of our festival prayer, 'Then shall the just see and be glad, the upright shall exult, the pious shall rejoice in song, and iniquity shall close its mouth, and all wickedness shall be wholly consumed like smoke, when Thou causest the dominion of arrogance to pass away from the earth...speedily, in our days!'

מוסף

Musaph

1. Collective Labour

If *avodah*, meaning 'labour' and 'worship,' is our general theme on these High Festivals, then we are reaching its very heart with the *Musaph* service about to begin. It contains a part simply called the *avodah*, the act of worship *par excellence*, describing the elaborate ritual of atonement performed by the High Priest in the Temple at Jerusalem.

In the course of this service we shall ourselves participate in a most unusual act. Three times, in addition to once during the *Aleinu*-prayer, we shall go down on our knees and prostrate ourselves before God, as we re-enact the impressive Temple service of old, when 'the priests and the people...hearing the ineffable Name pronounced by the High Priest in holiness and purity, knelt and prostrated themselves...and fell on their faces...'

Normally the Jew never kneels, neither before God nor before any mortal. Mordecai refused to kneel before the king in the Purim story, and Hannah of the *Chanukah* story had her seven sons slain rather than allow them to bow down before an idol even just to pick up a ring. Through the ages, Jews have always gone down to martyrdom rather than to their knees. Even in worshipping our God, kneeling, as a rule, is strictly forbidden. On the contrary, when reciting specially holy prayers, such as the *Shemoneh Esreh*, *Kaddish* or *Kedushah*, we are to stand erect and at attention before God, like soldiers inspected by their Commander-in-Chief. We even object to Jews ever kneeling casually in the course of work. Kneeling is both alien and abhorrent to the Jew, whether for a religious or any other purpose.

The sole exception is Rosh Hashanah and especially Yom Kippur. For once our ritual expects us to break the rule, to go down on our knees and prostrate ourselves in prayer. For once we are to return to the posture we had in the mother's womb before we were born, crouching on our knees in utter impotence and humiliation.

Does not this singular act symbolize the whole meaning of these Awesome Days? 'Thou turnest man back to dust (lit. a crushed state) and sayest: Return, ye children of man.'[86]

Unlike the animal, man is created to walk erect, to hold his head aloft, reaching for the skies above. Normally man strives and labours, thinks and creates, to raise himself, to climb the ladder of success, to reach out for wealth and power, to walk upright with pride and assurance through life.

Not so on these Days of Judgment and Atonement. Today we are to bend our knees and cringe, to recognize in utter humility the nothingness of man compared to the infinite and eternal majesty of God our Judge. Today we are to return to the embryonic state of pure innocence, to bite the dust in contrition and complete remorse. Today we are to kneel and lie prostrate before God, in humility and self-effacement.

The significance of this act goes even deeper.

What is the exception today will become the rule at the end of time. The time will come, as the Prophet has it, when 'every new moon and every Sabbath all flesh will come to bow down before Me, sayeth the Lord;'[87] and when, as we pray daily in the *Aleinu*-prayer, 'all inhabitants of the world will recognize and know that unto Thee every knee must bend and every tongue swear.'

Rosh Hashanah and Yom Kippur, then, give us a foretaste of things to come. What we do, what we feel, what we aspire to as a small people and as an exception today, will become the universal rule in the future. The time will come when every day will witness for all peoples the spiritual grandeur and complete submission to God we experience today.

These Days of Awe have other features, too, which for once bring close, and to the centre of our attention, experiences that otherwise still belong to the end.

For instance, the *Aleinu*-prayer itself, placed at the end of all services throughout the year, is on these days put right at the centre of *Musaph*, the central service of the day. Similarly, we wear today the *Kittel*, to be used as shrouds at the end of life to clothe our mortal remains after the departure of our immortal soul.

Our kneeling, our *Aleinu*, our *Kittel,* our complete dedication to God – all are exceptional and central today, but will become universal and the rule in the future. The atmosphere, the solemnity, the earnestness, the humility and faith of Rosh Hashanah and Yom Kippur will eventually be the common experience of all men every day. Man's corporate labour will be to worship and serve God in unison.

These are our objectives. What are the means to achieve them?

Time and again on this holy day, we have bent our heads and beaten our hearts while reciting the great confession of our sins: *Ashamnu, bagadnu, gazalnu...*'We have been guilty, we have dealt treacherously, we have robbed...,' and *Al chet shechatanu lephanecha begiluy arayoth, bzilzul horim umorim, bemasa uv'matan...*we have asked for forgiveness 'for the sin we have committed before Thee by immorality..., by despising parents and teachers ..., by dealings in business...'

Have we really committed this entire alphabetical catalogue of sins? Have we all been robbers, or shamed our parents and teachers, or been guilty of dishonest business practices? Or are our lips saying something our heart denies, turning us all into hypocrites and liars?

The answer is, of course, that Judaism holds us all corporately responsible for every crime committed in the society in which we live.

Man has rebelled against this notion from the beginning of history. The first question asked by man ever recorded in the Bible was: *Hashomer achi anochi*, 'Am I my brother's keeper?' And man has kept on asking this ever since.

We want to be individualists, to care only for ourselves, without bearing the burdens of others. We want to be left alone. But we cannot. *Lo tov heyoth ha'adam levado*, '**It is not good for man to be alone**,'[88] the world can never be good if man lives merely for himself alone, without any commitment to others.

Just as our personal life is influenced by the society and environment in which we live, so do we influence society around us. If there is stealing, or immorality, or disrespect for parents, or business dishonesty in the world today, we are all to blame and each one of us must beat his heart and say *Al chet*. We all belong to a collective labour force, as it were – as members of a community, of a nation, and of humanity; we are all our brothers' keepers, all responsible for one another.

On Rosh Hashanah we discussed how each of us benefits from the labours of others, how our lives are made better and easier through the creations and inventions and services of our neighbours and ancestors. But, to balance the account, we must also share in the blame for the faults and sins of others; we are degraded by the depravity of our neighbours.

Do you know which is the biggest business in America today? No, it is not General Motors or any of the other industrial giants. Crime is the largest business in the country today – a 200 hundred billion dollar per year business!

And we are all partners in this business, even if it may bring us more losses than profits. Crime needs a social climate in which to breed, and we all help to create that climate. Every time we look at a film glamorizing crime without protest, we encourage the popularization of crime and the vulgarization of life.

The other day our newspapers carried a heart-warming story about a man in Long Island who returned to its owner a precious dog he found and who refused a huge reward offered to him, arguing that he had only done what was right. For every such story of virtue in our papers there are 50 stories of crime and vice. If the ratio were reversed, we would soon secure a climate of moral health in which crime cannot become rampant.

Why is not the ratio reversed? Because we like to read about crime rather than about virtue; it is more exciting and entertaining. And the demand creates the supply.

Every time we allow ourselves to be entertained by crime, every time we buy a toy gun for a child, every time we are not too particular about business ethics, every time we offer a little graft, every time we act unkindly with workers or tenants, we encourage the rise of crime and become accessories to it.

The same goes for immorality, marital faithlessness and all the other vices so widespread today. By tolerating indecent exposure, by seeing films betraying the sanctity of marriage, by reading smutty literature, by ogling other men's wives, we help to corrode the fabric of our society and contribute to the loose morals of our age.

The same applies nearer home, to Jewish values.

For the first time in our history we now hear constantly talk about the 'vanishing Jew.' When persecution and slaughter decimated our people, no one ever spoke of the vanishing Jew. Throughout the Middle Ages, when the total number of Jews scarcely exceeded one million and whole communities were often bleeding to death or exposed to starvation, no Jew ever worried about the survival of his people. There was a wandering Jew, a suffering Jew, a martyred Jew, but never a vanishing Jew. And today, in our affluent and free society, where few Jews suffer hunger and none violent persecution or forced conversion, we lose them by the hundreds of thousands, through assimilation, mixed marriages and sheer indifference, combined with a record low birth-rate.

Orthodox Jews, it is true, who not so long ago were the vanishing tribe in America, are now probably the only segment of the community that, far from vanishing, increases through a relatively high birth-rate and a low assimilation rate. Nevertheless, we are all guilty partners to the crime of national suicide.

At present about 60,000 children attend Jewish day schools in America, while many times that number get no Jewish education at all. If these figures were reversed, the American Jew would not vanish!

If all Orthodox Jews – and not only the really charitable ones and the poor among them – were to tax themselves and spend ten per cent of their incomes on better Jewish education, we could accommodate in our day schools hundreds of thousands of children and give them enough education to ensure that they would not vanish. Our schools would not be dilapidated and overcrowded buildings disgracing the community, but palaces of learning; and our teachers would not suffer the hardship of going for months unpaid but, by earning a decent living, attract to their ranks men and women of the highest calibre now often lost to more lucrative pursuits.

Aval anachnu chatanu, 'but we have sinned.' We nibble at the problems of our time instead of labouring at them.

Our first order of the day, therefore, must be to restore our traditional sense of collective responsibility.

The criminal languishing in prison, the wretched partners to a broken marriage awaiting their release in a divorce court, the ignorant college student courting a non-Jewish girl and Jewish self-destruction — are all our brothers, and we are their keepers.

Yom Kippur wants to arouse in us this feeling of collective guilt, so that it paves the way to our collective happiness and security. Today we are sharing everything together, sinners and saints. No one has eaten better food than anybody else, no one has spent the day in more luxurious surroundings or enjoyed better entertainment than anyone else. We have all recited the same prayers, confessed the same sins, expressed the same hopes and pleaded for the same blessings.

But Yom Kippur is not an end in itself; it is but a guidepost to the future. What is an exception today is to become the rule tomorrow.

Let us learn today how to bend our knees before God in submission, how to wear the garb of death in the fullness of life, how to beat our own hearts for the sins of others. Then we may soon see realized the triple programme for the future outlined in the threefold prayer characterizing these Days of Awe: First, the brotherhood of man: 'And impose Thine awe upon all Thy works...that they may fear Thee and all creatures prostrate themselves before Thee, that they may all form a single band to do Thy will with a perfect heart...' Second, turning the vanishing Jew into the vanquishing Jew, jubilant in his spiritual triumph: 'And give glory unto Thy people, praise to them that fear Thee, hope to them that seek Thee... joy to Thy land and gladness to Thy city...' And third, the victory of righteousness and the extinction of crime: 'And the righteous shall see and rejoice...while iniquity shall close her mouth, and all evil shall be wholly consumed like smoke...,' *Bimherah beyameinu*, 'speedily, in our days!'

2. Farewell to my Congregation

In my Odyssey of *Lech Lecha* – my sermon-theme on these Days of Awe – I have moved *me'artzecha umimoldtecha*, from my country and my community, to reach now the climax of my wrench *mibeth avicha*, from my synagogue-family, from my congregation.

Many of you may remember the most joyful personal occasion I celebrated with you – the Bar Mitzvah of my first-born son. In launching him to independence as a Jew in his own right, I cited the introduction to the blessing our father Jacob gave his children before his departure: 'Gather together, and I will tell you what will happen to you in the end of days' (Gen. 49:1), and I gave him Rashi's explanation: 'He sought to reveal the end, but the Divine Presence departed from him, and he began talking about other matters.'

As a father, I would wish to tell my child what is in store for him, I would want to reveal the future to him. But a veil of secrecy is drawn over my vision, and I must talk about other matters.

Similarly, my congregation, I wished in blessing you on this last Yom Kippur together, I could reveal your future to you. I wished I could tell you what is in store for you; whether the seeds planted here during the past eight years will prosper and bear fruit or not; whether you will meet with success or failure, with joys or sorrows. Alas, I cannot, for Providence hides the future from me as from you, and I must turn to other matters than prognosticating the future.

All I can do in blessing you is, as Jacob and countless Jewish fathers did in blessing their children, to tell you what you *should* be, and what I, as your spiritual leader since your congregational birth, tried to achieve and make of you.

THE THREE FUNCTIONS OF A CONGREGATION

In Hebrew we use three distinct terms for 'congregation': *edah* or *adath*, *kahal* or *kehillah*, and *tzibbur*. Each term describes a different aspect of what a Jewish congregation is to stand for, and each is usually linked with a different word for its leader, likewise describing a distinct task facing a congregational leader:

Edah is associated in the Torah with *zaken*, 'elder,' as in the frequent combination of *ziknei ha-edah* 'the elders of the congregation.' *Kahal* is usually connected with *rosh*, 'head,' when we speak of a *rosh ha-kahal*, 'the head of a congregation.' And *tzibbur* is used with *shali'ach*, 'messenger' or 'representative,' as in *shali'ach tzibbur*, 'the congregation's agent.'

Of course, these three terms for leader commonly denote three different persons leading the community. *Zaken*, 'elder', stands for *zeh shekanah chochmah*, the scholar, the rabbi, the spiritual leader. *Rosh ha-kahal* is used for the lay leader, the president or *parnas* who secures the material or administrative needs of the congregation. And *shali'ach tzibbur* is the *chazan*, and the messenger of the congregation who leads and conveys their prayers as the representative of the worshippers.

However, in a broader sense, all these terms may be applied to the rabbi as defining his functions of spiritual leadership, just as the three terms for congregation describe the three purposes of a community.

THE TESTIMONY OF A CONGREGATION

Edah derives from *ed*, 'witness' or *eduth* 'testimony.' It is also connected with *mo'ed*, 'appointed season' or 'festival'.

The first function of a Jewish congregation is to be a witness, to bear testimony, to the truth of our faith. In Jewish law no *ed echad,* no 'single witness,' however unimpeachable, can ever be a legal witness at court. In charges against an individual, or in validating legal acts, we must have at least two witnesses, *al pi shnayim edim*. In publicly bearing testimony to God, in *kiddush ha-Shem* – sanctifying His Name, we require more. *Edah* means at least a *minyan*, ten Jews.

No single Jew. however eminent or pious, can ever proclaim the message of Judaism, can ever hallow His Name, as effectively as can any ten Jews worshipping together, however common they are.

Pious, observant Jews have been living in this area as individuals for many years. But the history of Orthodoxy, of bearing witness to the vitality of traditional Judaism in this select district, only began with the foundation of our synagogue.

Our first and foremost task, then, as I saw it, was to be an *edah*, a corporate witness testifying that traditional Judaism is very much alive, and confounding the Prophets of doom who forecast long ago that Orthodoxy could not survive in America, certainly not amid the affluence, elegance and modernity of an area as fashionable as ours. I am proud and happy that in this objective we have largely succeeded, in part beyond our wildest dreams. We have demonstrated a *kiddush ha-Shem* in the most public manner for the world to see.

No one, anywhere will ever again be able to say that strict Orthodoxy is incompatible with modern life, that our unadulterated traditions are only for foreigners and old-fashioned people, that you cannot reach the top of the economic ladder and still remain faithful to all our ancient convictions and practices.

We are the *edim*, 'witnesses', to prove that it can be done, that Judaism can flourish in Fifth Avenue as in Williamsburg or Jerusalem, in the twentieth century as a 100 or a 1,000 years ago.

THE RABBI AS TEACHER

It is in association with *edah* that spiritual leaders are called *zekenim*, 'elders' or 'scholars'. My task in helping this congregation to become an *edah* was to present to you, and through you to the community at large, the magnificent vistas of Jewish learning, some insights into Jewish scholarship, to enhance the appreciation for the Jewish faith and observances. I regarded my principal assignment here as being your teacher, so that through knowledge you would be truthful witnesses. For, on what you do not know for sure, you cannot give evidence.

These tasks, yours as an *edah* and mine as a *zaken*, we tried to fulfil together at our *mo'adim*, the 'appointed times' when we came together for worship and study, at our services and classes.

Of course, a lot remains to be accomplished. To be an *edah*, a corporate witness to God on earth, every member of the congregation must display an adequate knowledge and observance of Judaism. '**For this is your wisdom and your understanding in the eyes of the nations, that when they hear all these laws, they shall say "What a wise and understanding nation is this great people?"**' (Deut. 4:6). A real *adath ha-Shem* brings the *Shechinah* down to earth:

Elokim nitzav ba'adath El, 'God is established in the congregation of the Lord' (Ps. 82:1). Such a congregation makes God manifest among all who enter it, makes them sense the mystic spell of the Divine.

Our success or failure as an *edah,* and mine as its *zaken,* cannot be measured by how many people attended our services or paid us compliments, but ultimately by how many worshippers we inspired to discover God in their souls, faith in their hearts, the thrill of Torah learning in their minds, and the beauty of Mitzvah performance in their deeds. The true test to prove whether we are an *edah* is whether we served as an example to other congregations, whether we have helped to intensify Jewish education, to support charitable causes, to contribute to the well-being and religious vitality of the wider community.

What congregation anywhere has a greater opportunity, more fame and resources to achieve these goals than ours?

A congregation thinking only of itself and its own welfare defaults in its obligations no less than a selfish individual who is unconcerned with the needs of others. To bear testimony, to be a witness, you must convince others, you must carry a jury – or Jewry, in our case – with you. You must serve the public and impersonal cause of justice and truth, of spreading the rule of God and morality.

THE TOGETHERNESS OF A CONGREGATION

Next, a congregation is also called *kahal* or *kehillah,* literally 'a gathering' of people. Here the emphasis is on the congregation as an instrument for welding individuals into a community.

The second principal task of a congregation is to give each member a sense of belonging, a loyalty to a larger group, a feeling of togetherness.

THE RABBI AS HEAD

In relation to this function of a congregation, its leader is called *rosh*, 'head'. Just as the head, with its brain and nerve-centre, governs the functions of all organs and limbs, and co-ordinates their movements and activities, so must the rabbi bind the members together to make them feel they belong to one body, he must co-ordinate their thinking and their acting to serve the interest of that body in unison and harmony.

In good measure, we certainly succeeded in creating an intimate fellowship of a closely knit family, but in part the task is far from fulfilled.

The Torah uses the word *kahal* most prominently in the Sidrah bearing the very name *Vayakhel*, when Moses 'congregated' the people to announce the Sabbath laws to be observed 'in all their habitations' (Ex. 35:1–3). Rashi comments that this occurred 'on the morrow of Yom Kippur'.

The real test of strength of a congregation as a *kahal* is not on Yom Kippur, when the synagogue is packed, not on the *mo'adim* at our festive services, but on the following day. The test is determined by how much of Yom Kippur's spirit carries over to the day after, how far our synagogue services on the *mo'adim* influence our home life and hallow our Sabbath observance 'in all our habitations'. A true congregation does not consist of joint prayers and studies only, but of cementing a partnership, a brotherhood of togetherness, which makes the members remember that they belong to a synagogue even on the day after they attended an inspiring service; which disciplines them to serve God at home or in the office, at work or at leisure, just as devoutly as in the synagogue; and which makes them worry about the congregation's affairs and problems as about their own business.

In serving as your *rosh,* I endeavoured to influence your thoughts and feelings, to direct your movements and to co-ordinate your activities even when you were away from our sanctuary. My greatest joy was when I heard that through my teachings some home had become kosher; some people had given up working or riding in the Sabbath; some parents had sent their child to a yeshivah; some boy had taken a worthy Jewish girl to be his wife; or some member had volunteered his services to the congregation.

THE INDIVIDUALS OF A CONGREGATION

Finally, a congregation is a *tzibbur,* from *tzavar,* 'to make a heap'. This stresses neither the lofty testimony of the *edah* nor the togetherness of the *kahal;* rather it stands for the wants of the individual, the services the congregation renders to each member in his personal needs.

Tzibbur is made up of the initials for *Tzaddikim,* 'righteous people', *Beynonim*, 'indifferent people', and *Resha'im*, 'wicked people'. For every community, if you dissect it into its constituent parts, is a heap of saints, sinners and in-betweens.

THE RABBI AS AGENT

Its leader is called *shali'ach*, 'messenger' or 'representative'. For the rabbi must act as the agent of them all, and feel equally close to each of them in their troubles and joys. In this capacity it was my charge to intercede for you when sickness struck, to comfort you in grief, to cheer you in anxiety and to advise you in perplexity, as well as to sanctify your family events, to celebrate your births and Bar Mitzvahs and weddings – to be God's spokesman in your midst and your spokesman before God.

There is little that gave me more gratification than the occasions I had to rejoice with you, or to dry some tear on a care-worn face, or to bring some smile to a patient on the sickbed. In this work there was no difference between sinner and saint or the average in-between. I tried to pray as hard for the daily worshipper as for the person I saw only once a year. All are equally part of the *tzibbur*, and I was responsible equally to be their *shali'ach*.

I was proud to be your *shali'ach* in another sense, too. In all my hundreds of lectures and addresses all over the land, in all my attendances at communal meetings and national conventions, in all my activities on various organization boards and committees, and in all my writings in books and magazines, I appeared as your representative. I was introduced as your rabbi or greeted as your spiritual leader. The Fifth Avenue Synagogue was the prestigious platform that always travelled with me, even as the White House travels with the President wherever he goes.

I began this series with *lech lecha…mibeth avicha.* This phrase 'father's house' occurs again two generations after Abraham. On fleeing from his home, Jacob vowed his tribute to God if *veshavti veshalom el beth avi,* 'I return in peace to my father's house' (Gen. 28:21). I likewise pray that from time to time I may return to this congregational family of mine and find them *beshalom*, in peace with one another, and in peace with God. May I come to find you, as was said of my namesake Jacob, *vayavo Ya'akov shalem,* 'And Jacob came in peace' (Gen. 33:18), literally 'in perfection' or 'completeness', as explained by Rashi: 'Perfect in body, perfect in possessions, and perfect in Torah.'

נעילה

Neilah

1. The Pangs of Labour

> It is the day of atonement; a holy convocation shall
> it be unto you, and ye shall afflict yourselves.[89]

Our most exacting spiritual labours of the year, which began on Labour Day, are about to be concluded. We have traced the concept of labour from our service to God to the services of others to us, from the labour of the rabbi to the collective labour of the community.

Now, as the pain of hunger begins to torment us in these final moments of the fast, we shall turn to the pangs of labour.

Suffering is the inevitable concomitant of all service and creation.

When the first man and woman were created and placed in the Garden of Eden to work and guard it, they sinned. They, and all their descendants after them, were punished for what they had done in opening the floodgates of sin to the entire human race. Adam was told: 'Cursed be the ground for they sake; in pain shalt thou eat of it...thorns and thistles shall it bring forth for thee...In the sweat of they face shalt thou eat bread...' And Eve was told: 'I will greatly multiply thy pain and thy travail; in pain shalt thou bring forth children...'[90]

Both of them would suffer the pangs of labour in bringing forth new creation: the man outside in labouring to produce bread, and the woman inside in labouring to deliver children.

From the beginning, then, it was ordained that nothing would be created by man or woman without sweat and pain. Neither the life of a new plant sustaining human existence nor the life of a new child propagating the human race could be produced without suffering. There could be no true creation without travail.

Is not this one of the great lessons of Yom Kippur?

Today we have endured affliction; we have denied our hungry and thirsty bodies the balm of food and drink. That is surely the very reason why we were creative today. Our personalities are reborn in the pangs of labour, the pain of self-affliction.

If any day of the year changes us, makes some difference to our character, it is surely this day. We are purged of the burden of sin, morally and spiritually regenerated to assume a new and more meaningful life. This refining process can no more be accomplished without suffering than metal can be refined without heat or children be born without pangs.

Is this not also one of the great lessons of Jewish history?

When a son was born to Joseph in Egypt – the first Jew to taste the experience of exile from his homeland – he called him Ephraim, explaining *Ki hiphrani Elokim be'eretz onyi*, 'for the Lord that made me fruitful in the land of my affliction.'[91] Affliction made him fruitful and creative. And when later all his family went down to Egypt and they experienced the first blows of persecution in our history, we are told of the nascent Jewish people: *V'cha'asher y'anu otho ken yirbeh v'chen yifrotz*, 'and the more they oppressed it, the more it multiplied and spread.'[92] Oppression made Israel prolific.

And so it was throughout our history. Suffering produced an irresistible will to create new life and immortal monuments to the human genius. We became at once the most suffering and the most creative people on earth.

'If there are ranks in suffering,' wrote the great German-Jewish scholar Zunz in a celebrated passage quoted by George Eliot in *Daniel Deronda*:

Israel takes precedence of all nations; if the duration of sorrows and the patience with which they are borne ennoble, the Jews can challenge the aristocracy of every land; if a literature is called rich in the possession of a few classic tragedies – what shall we say to a national tragedy lasting 1500 years, in which the poets and the actors were also the heroes?

Compare the number of Jewish Prophets and philosophers, of Jewish Nobel Prize winners and other world-renowned benefactors of mankind, to the number produced by any other people of the same size, and the lesson becomes indisputable.

Is not this also one of the great lessons of life itself?

According to a famous talmudic witticism *Asya dimagen b'magen, magen shavya,* 'a doctor who heals for nothing is worth nothing.'[93] Indeed, anything you get for nothing is worth nothing. Only what is won the hard way is truly treasured.

Just as a mother loves her child all the more because she bore it with pain and sacrifice, and as a man will cherish his accomplishments all the more dearly if he achieved them by the sweat of his brow, so does our appreciation for anything in life rise in proportion to the hardship we endured in gaining it.

Children do not appreciate food or candies if they do not occasionally hunger for them. A student will not feel the thrill of passing an examination if he did not sweat for it. A person will not really be attached to a charity, to a hospital or a Yeshivah or any other noble cause, unless it has meant a sacrifice of time and money to him, nor will he love his synagogue if he obtained its services for nothing. For this reason the Torah insists that pilgrims visiting the Temple 'shall not appear before the Lord empty', without offerings.[94]

Yom Kippur would not pull our heart-strings if we had not fasted and afflicted ourselves, and the Prophet Jonah would not have addressed Nineveh with such passion if he had not experienced the terror of the storm at sea on his way there.

And so it is also with religion in general. A religion which demands nothing is worth nothing.

How else can we explain that Orthodox Judaism, which is so hard to practice, loses far fewer Jews than non-Orthodoxy, which is so much easier to non-practice.

What you work hard for you love, and out of travail you create. Modern Israel, so uniquely creative, is an unmatched example of pioneering in the work for the very reason that it was born and raised in the torment of fire and sweat. 'Those who sow in tears will reap in joy.'[95]

True happiness is catapulted from the stresses of effort and struggle. The forthcoming festival of Succot would not be 'the season of our joy,' if it were not preceded by the exertions of Rosh Hashanah and Yom Kippur.

Our Sages state that when Yom Kippur terminates one should rejoice and be of good cheer. In anticipating the conclusion of this great day, let me close our series on labour in a lighter vein, with a story on today's biggest labour problem – domestic labour.

A letter was once published in the advice-giving column of a newspaper from a woman with a problem. Her husband snored all night, and she could not sleep. Otherwise, she admitted, he was kind and considerate. He even provided her with two maids to help her with housework. But his snoring irritated her, resulting in her loss of sleep. And she was nervous all day. What, she asked, should she do?

The columnist replied: 'My dear woman, send away the maids and do the housework yourself. You will then be so tired at night that your husband will not disturb your sleep.'

Some of us have a similar problem in a spiritual sense. They have the labour of Judaism performed by maids, by others who keep the household of God running all year round, while they themselves take it easy. They let their synagogues organize adult classes and services, but they want others to attend them. Then, through the snoring voice of their conscience, they are unable to find peace of mind, and when they awaken to the brilliant daylight of Rosh Hashanah and Yom Kippur, and attend services, they tend to become nervous, fumble in the *Machzor*, and are unable to follow the services. What should they do?

The answer is: Work hard at Judaism by yourself, and not by proxy, all the year round. Make an effort to keep a truly kosher home, sanctify the Sabbath, come regularly to services, give up at least one night a week for Jewish studies. You will then be so preoccupied that the snores of your conscience will be silenced at night and you will not be in any state of nervousness in the presence of God by day.

'When thou eatest the labour of thine own hands, happy shalt thou be and it shall be well with thee.'[96] May our exacting labour today and our Jewish work throughout the year ensure for us a year blessed with every happiness and well-being!

2. Leaving in Peace

We have now reached the hour of *Ne'ilah*, 'the closing of the gates.' With it, our journey, which began on Rosh Hashanah with *lech lecha* and passed through *artzecha*, *moladtecha* and *beth avicha*, will come to an end.

At this moment of climax and conclusion, of closing and parting, what should our feelings be? Sadness that the great experience we had together is over? Or anxiety lest our spiritual efforts did not succeed? Or fear of what the future may bring to us? No, none of these emotions are in place at this hour.

We read earlier today about the unique Yom Kippur service in the Temple of old, conducted entirely by the High Priest. His was a responsibility and a privilege shared by no other Jew. After an exacting 24-hour-long round of ritual functions and vigil, he entered, alone, just this once a year, the Holy of Holies in the Temple, in order there to make atonement 'for himself, for his family, and for all the congregation of Israel.' On him rested the terrible burden of securing forgiveness for an entire people, of pleading for their welfare, and of guiding their spiritual destiny. This was his moment of truth and supreme challenge, as he stood there, alone with God, on the holiest day of the year, and on the holiest spot on earth, where Abraham was once prepared to sacrifice his 'only son Isaac,' the spot towards which Jews everywhere and at all times have turned in prayer ever since then.

The burdens of the High Priest were so heavy, and the strains and tensions so great, that people feared for his safety. Since no one else was ever permitted to enter the Holy of Holies, they attached chains to the High Priest before he went in, so that he could be pulled outside if anything happened to him whilst he was inside.

Now, how did he feel when the service was over, when he safely emerged from his spiritual ordeal in the Holy of Holies? Sad that it had come to an end? Or anxious lest he did not succeed? Or fearful of what the future might bring? No, our sources tell us, as we read in our *Machzor* today: 'And the High Priest made a *Yom Tov* party for his friends after he had entered in peace (into the Holy of Holies) and came out in peace without incident.' He was jubilant, joyfully thanking God for the privilege to lead and represent His people before Him, and for passing through his grave responsibilities in peace and without harm.

I feel likewise at this moment. A rabbi in spiritual charge of a congregation, especially in our turbulent times, carries a crushing burden. His is a high privilege, but also an awesome responsibility. If he can emerge from a term of office serving figuratively in the Holy of Holies, and say 'I have entered in peace and I have come out in peace without incident,' then he has indeed reason to be jubilant and to celebrate a special *Yom Tov*.

At this hour of *Ne'ilah*, therefore, I joyfully thank God for the honour He bestowed upon me in guiding you, for protecting me from all strife and enmity, for letting me go out in peace as I came in in peace. At this moment I plead for forgiveness for any wrongs I may have done you, and for God's forgiveness and atonement to me, to my family and to all my congregation for the offences we committed against Him and our fellow men.

The laws of Yom Kippur conclude with the following paragraph: 'There is a Midrash stating that on the termination of Yom Kippur a Heavenly voice goes forth and says: "Go and eat your bread in joy and drink your wine with a happy heart, for God has already accepted your works"' (Eccl. 9:7) (*Kitzur Shulchan Aruch*, 133:29).

May God's blessings of peace and joy always be with you as a holy congregation ennobling the entire House of Israel.

Notes to sermons

The following first appeared in *Journal of a Rabbi* (London: W.H. Allen, 1967): The Blessings of Fear; 'With All Thine Heart' – The Meaning of Prayer; The Human Rights Revolution; 'For Man is Born to Labour'; The Scientific Revolution; 'With All Thy Mind' – Our Belief in God; The Religious Revolution; The Burdens of the Rabbi's Labour; Reflections on the Jewish Concept of After-life; 'With All Thy Might' – Ethics and Religion; The Moral Revolution; Collective Labour; The Pangs of Labour; Leaving in Peace.

The following first appeared in *The Timely and the Timeless: Homiletical Memories of America* (London: Vallentine Mitchell, 1977): Farewell to my Congregation.

1. Amos 36:6–8.
2. *Sanhedrin* 4:5.
3. Ps. 20:8.
4. Gen. 48:22.
5. E. Munk, *The World of Prayer*, 1954, p. 1.
6. Ps. 34:19.
7. 102:1.
8. *Kitzur Shulchan Aruch*, 128:7.
9. Bezalel Landau, 'Prayer in the Teaching of Chasidism', in *Or Hamizrach*, September 1960, p. 57, in the name of the Maggid of Koznitz.
10. *Gen. Rabba*, 45:5.
11. Gen. 30:1.
12. I Sam. 1:10.
13. *Yevamoth* 64b.
14. *Ta'anith* 8a.
15. Quoted by S.A. Horodetsky, *Leaders of Hasidism*, 1928, p. 94.
16. *Ta'anith* 2a.
17. Ephraim Lencziez, *Amudei Shesh*, 1617, p. 23c.
18. *Or Hamizrach*, op. cit., p. 55ff.
19. *Or Hamizrach*, op. cit., p. 53ff.
20. Quoted by M. Samuel, *Prince of the Ghetto*, 1948, p. 162.
21. Jonah 3:1–10.
22. Malachi 2:10.
23. *Sanhedrin* 4:5.
24. Hos. 4:9; *Shabbath* 119b.
25. *New York Times*, 9 September 1963.

26. Job. 5:7.
27. Gen. 2:15.
28. *Ethics of the Fathers*, 2:15.
29. *Orach Chayim*, 231.
30. Deut. 7:12–15.
31. Deut. 30:26.
32. Deut. 16:14.
33. Deut. 4:6, *Shabbath* 75a.
34. *Orach Chayim*, 224:7.
35. Ps. 19:2.
36. A week after delivering this sermon, I found some of these thoughts re-echoed in 'Skeptical Look at "Scientific Experts"' by David E. Lilienthal, *The New York Times Magazine*, 29 September 1963: 'The evidence increases that we are in the midst of a crisis in the scientific community...The crisis of confidence has its roots in concern that scientists and other experts...have more and more been seeking to use methods applicable to the physical world in areas of the world of men that are beyond the reach of such methods: human goals and purposes ... Many of the most noted of these experts and specialists have departed from their own fields of competence with a cocksure confidence that they can find answers – out of their scientific or technical knowledge or intuition – to what cannot be finally and firmly answered at all...'
37. *Gen. Rab.*, 1:10; *Tanchuma Yashan, Yithro*, 16.
38. Is. 27:13.
39. Deut. 6:5.
40. 19:2.
41. *Shulchan Aruch, Orach Chayim*, 42:1.
42. Alfred North Whitehead, *Science and the Modern World*, 1960, p. 13.
43. J.W.N. Sullivan, *The Limitations of Science*, 1959, p. 94.
44. Gen. 15:5, 19:2.
45. Fred Hoyle, *Frontiers of Astronomy*, 1960, p. 52.
46. *Emunoth Vede'oth*, 3:7.
47. Micah 6:8.
48. Jer. 31:17.
49. Deut. 32:4.
50. Gen. 4:1.
51. Hos. 2:21–22.
52. Zech. 14:7.
53. *Hil. Teshuvah*, 3:4.

54. *Horayoth* 10b.
55. Eccl. 9:7; *Kitzur Shulchan Aruch*, 133:29.
56. Ps. 82:3.
57. *Yalkut Shimoni*, 2:831.
58. Is. 55:10–11.
59. *Ethics of the Fathers*, 4:21, 22.
60. Nu. 23:10; cf. *Sanhedrin* 105a.
61. I Sam. 25:29.
62. Eccl. 12:7.
63. Ps. 16:10.
64. See Y.M. Tucatzinski, *Gesher Ha-Chayim* (*Bridge of Life*). Jerusalem 1960, part 3, pp. 5 ff.
65. Eccl. 7:1.
66. *Ethics of the Fathers*, 4:21, 22.
67. Maimonides, *Mishnah Commentary*, *Sanhedrin*, Ch. X (introduction).
68. *Berachoth* 17a.
69. Is. 25:8.
70. Is. 58:5–7.
71. *Berachoth* 6b.
72. *Sanhedrin* 35a.
73. See Rashi, on Gen. 47:29.
74. Max Otto, *Science and the Moral Life*, 1958, p. 37.
75. Nachman of Kasovir, quoted by J.J. Katz, *Toldoth Jakov Joseph*, 1903, p. 39ff.
76. Ps. 17:19; *Bava Bathra* 10a.
77. Is. 58:8–9.
78. *Erachin* 15b.
79. Jer. 6:13.
80. Ibid., 14.
81. Maim., *Hil. Issurei Bi'ah*, 19:17.
82. Lev. 19:17.
83. *Bava Bathra* 12a.
84. Ps. 49:18.
85. Num. 11:29.
86. Ps. 90:3.
87. Is. 66:23.
88. Gen. 2:18.
89. Lev. 23:27.
90. Gen. 3:17–19.

91. Gen. 41:52.
92. Ex. 1:12.
93. *Bava Kamma* 85a.
94. Deut. 16:16.
95. Ps. 126:5.
96. Ps. 128:2.

BROADCASTS

III
Broadcasts

By a tradition almost as old as religious broadcasting, the BBC has allotted 15 minutes twice a year to successive Chief Rabbis for seasonal talks prior to every Rosh Hashanah and Passover. Lately some of these programmes have been varied to include occasional interviews and discussions on Jewish religious topics.

1. Creation and Judgement*

The message of Rosh Hashanah, though thousands of years old, has never been more relevant than in our turbulent age. The Festival combines two distinct aspects: it traditionally marks the anniversary of the creation of the world, as described in the Book of Genesis; and we also observe it as the Day of Judgement before God. On the one hand, it proclaims our *origin* as children of God, and on the other hand, our *destiny* as having to render an account for our actions.

The fact that we are the product not of chance but of choice, that we exist by design and not by accident, renders us liable to judgement. For only that which is deliberately created can be asked why and for what purpose it exists and whether it has fulfilled the intentions of its creator.

Our age is witnessing new creation on a scale more vast and dramatic than ever before. Whether the convulsive events around us represent the death agony of a dying civilization or the birth pangs of a new era, they certainly indicate the most momentous change from one order to another ever seen in a single generation.

---

*New Year Broadcast, 1968

The year we are just concluding in the Jewish calendar has made an especially massive contribution to fanning the storms of change. It was a year in which we heard, as at every birth of new life, much crying; it was an exceptionally noisy year. Throughout the year we heard a cacophony of deafening sounds and shrieks: the murderous bombs and mortar shells exploding in war-torn Vietnam; the rumbling of invading tanks brutally crushing a brave people gasping for freedom; the heart-rending groans of Biafran children starving to death; the shattering explosions of terrorist mines ripping peaceful civilians in Israel, and the nearby cries of despair from Arab refugees drained of all human dignity in the world's worst breeding grounds of hate; assassins' shots snuffing out the lives of great world leaders; the confused din of wild demonstrations against universities and governments and other assorted symbols of authority or discipline; not to forget the world-wide chorus of fierce press campaigns to drown out the ancient voice of ecclesiastical fiat.

Of course, history never stood still or mute. The world always recreated itself, with change as the only really constant factor in the human experience. But what has changed is the speed of change. Today there are more changes and innovations in a single lifetime than previously in the whole of recorded human history. For instance, it is estimated that we now double the sum total of scientific knowledge about the universe we live in as was previously accumulated in all the millennia of man's search for knowledge since the dawn of history. In other spheres, too, the acceleration of change is hardly less extreme. Within the last couple of decades we have certainly seen greater changes in some of our religious, moral, social and scientific thinking than had previously occurred in many centuries of slow evolution. Nowadays we all occupy grandstand seats to watch – at closer range than ever before – the birth of a new world, the creation of a new order.

This is where the twin meaning of our New Year comes in. In the Jewish view there can be no creation without judgement. Even God Himself judged what He had created: 'And God saw all that He had made, and behold it was very good,' as we read at the end of the creation story in Genesis. Hence, the dividing line between the old year and the new one to which it gives birth is the Day of Judgement. How much more so when an entire era expires to pass on the gift of life to a new era.

The knowledge that there must be judgement safeguards the new creation from crippling malformation or premature death. How many fatal blunders, how much misery and failure, could be avoided if only we remembered our liability to ultimate judgement before we act, if only we associated the risk of every creation with the certainty of being judged eventually! Recent events in the world's two mightiest seats of power in the East and in the West provide sad and dramatic evidence. If the Eastern bloc rulers had been aware that they would one day be held to account by their own people for their inhuman betrayal of their Czechoslovak allies just as surely as Stalin was brought to judgement for his crimes and political blunders by his successors, would they not have shrunk back from their cynical abuse of power? And if the Free World's leading ruler had realized in time that the massive judgement before the bar of history would compel him to bow out of his exalted office, might he not have listened to the cooing of the doves at least as sympathetically as to the crying of the hungry hawks?

The same surely applies to all of us, at whatever level of life or society, whether we sit in the cockpit of leadership at the controls in man's flight through history, or we are seated further back as mere passengers, watching the panorama of life fleeting by beneath us. Only by the constant realization that a judgement awaits us can we ensure that we use our talents and energies to create and not to destroy. Only by remembering always that we are accountable for all our actions, that life is not meant to be just an idle pursuit of carefree relaxation and amusement, can we avoid the irredeemable tragedy of wasted lives, of leaving this world without enriching it, or worse still of impeding man's progress to his destination.

We talked of creation and judgement. Judgement before whom? Who is to judge what to create and what to destroy, what to discard of the old world and what to contrive for the new? Here, too, the symbolism of our New Year is to provide the answer. On this solemn Day of Judgement we shall blow the *Shofar*, the ram's horn, at our Divine services. This ram's horn is to remind us of the ram which once replaced Isaac's sacrifice marking the birth of Judaism, or indeed the genesis of monotheism, the belief in God and the brotherhood of man. Nearly 500 years later the ram's horn was sounded at Mount Sinai, heralding the proclamation of the Ten Commandments and the revelation of God's law to the Children of Israel, at the birth of the moral order which has governed the progress of human civilization ever since. This ram's horn is a simple, unsophisticated musical instrument which has not changed over the ages. We use it to usher in every New Year, as a reminder that everything we create and achieve will ultimately be judged by the timeless truths which are as valid today as when they were discovered by Abraham and revealed to Moses.

Lately we hear increasingly about a new voice, called the voice of our conscience, competing with the voice of religion as the judge to determine what is right and what is wrong, to define the difference between good and evil. If you are in any doubt, we are told, on what the moral law requires, for instance, on the complex moral questions involved in heart-transplants or in abortions, or on intimate relationships outside marriage and how many children to have inside it, then just consult your conscience and you will have the answer. The clamour today is to worship not God but our conscience, and when the two conflict, let the conscience prevail.

Judaism, as a reliable guide to human conduct, looks elsewhere; it relies no more on the natural law than on the individual conscience. We believe the rules of the moral law can only be established by God as our Supreme Judge; they are not enshrined in any laws of nature or in the capricious whims of the human conscience. If we are really honest with ourselves, don't we often use our conscience merely as a convenient expedient to justify our self-interest? And do not the judgements of our conscience vary with every age and from one individual to another? How reliable can the conscience be when, as we are told, it now tells many priests and other deeply religious people to reject moral teachings to which only ten years ago their conscience demanded conformity with equal insistence?

Is the conscience not often fickle, swayed by the slightest winds of popular propaganda and personal desire, and easily perverted? In our permissive society the conscience tells thousands of young people that they can shape and twist the moral code to their own specifications, so long as they do it in the name of true love and happiness. Behind the Iron Curtain millions are sincerely convinced by their consciences, after adequate indoctrination, that the freedom of the individual must be sacrificed for the good of the state or the social system, and I have little doubt that many Nazis had genuinely believed they were carrying out the dictates of their conscience when they shoved millions of people into gas chambers to promote their insane doctrines of racial purity.

Of course we cherish the refined conscience as man's noblest possession, so long as it is but the instrument through which the Divine composition of virtue and goodness is being played out. As an inner power stronger than any army or police force, the conscience is meant to keep us away from the brink of evil and temptation and to urge us on to acts of righteousness and moral bravery. It is the very essence of our religious belief that the conscience serves not to *make* moral laws but to *enforce* them. We need our conscience not to tell us what is right but, knowing what is right, to make us act accordingly. This is symbolized by the ancient ram's horn, breaking the sound-barriers of time by transmitting to us the echoes of God's voice rebounding from the mountains of Moriah and Sinai. Truth, virtue, honesty and other moral values, though subject to reinterpretation as circumstances change, would be worthless if they did not speak with the same authentic accents in all ages and to every human society, just as the laws of nature are immutable even if our growing understanding and application of them constantly expand the frontiers of science and technology.

It is this stability in the midst of change, this firm judgement in the adventure of creation, which invests true religion with majesty, guiding like a fixed star in the firmament our storm-tossed ship of life across the ocean of history to its ultimate destination.

According to the Jewish tradition, this same ram's horn will also be sounded to proclaim our eventual redemption, the time when all men will acclaim God as their Judge and their conscience as His law-enforcement agent, when every man will see his own happiness in the happiness of his neighbour, the time when 'nation shall not lift up sword against nation, neither shall they learn war any more.' May this New Year speed the realization of this unchanging dream of the ages. May it bring freedom to the oppressed, equality to the deprived, peace to those pursued by war and terror, relief to the sick in body, soul or mind, inspiration to all leaders of men, and the joy of fulfilment to Creator and creatures alike.

2. Reaching the Moon: Two Perspectives*

The date for the beginning of our year, just like the beginning of every Hebrew month, is fixed to coincide with the New Moon. On this New Year's eve, we may truly speak of the New Moon in a special sense. For new indeed is the moon bearing the footprints of man on its surface, and equally new are the expanded vistas gained by man's spectacular ascent into the heavens, though different evaluations and appraisals may emerge from this conquest of space.

Some have already hailed the moon adventure as the greatest enterprise in the history of man, easily worth the billions of dollars spent on its accomplishment and eclipsing every previous epoch-making event across the expanse of the centuries. But there are others to whom this colossal enterprise appears to be the most extravagant wastage of human and material resources, an enterprise of which they may say: 'Never has so much been contributed by so many for so little.' Of course, the many-faceted truth is that there is a measure of validity in both conflicting evaluations. There can be no doubt but that man's successfully reaching for the moon represents both the most glorious tribute of all times to human ingenuity, vision, courage and the quest for knowledge, and, at the same time, possibly the most gigantic monument to vainglorious national ambition, reaching a peak of irrelevance in the context of our earthly problems.

Of infinitely greater significance, however, is a similar divergence of judgement in assessing the present state of our terrestrial world around us from the perspective of the moon.

I well recall a fascinating sermon published nearly a decade ago in the American *Reader's Digest*, giving an imaginary

---

*New Year Broadcast, 1969.

account of what the first man to set foot on the moon would see and experience. The spaceman had landed on the powdery surface of the moon, gazed in wonderment and overpowering solitude at the primeval desolation around him, completed his scientific chores, and then, during a moment of contemplation, heard this message in the silence of his soul:

> 'You, Astronaut of Earth, are now standing upon an uncontaminated celestial body. Across these dusty plains and in these towering mountains there is not, and never has been, the slightest stain of sin or evil. No lie has yet been told in this silent world. These rocks are unstained by the blood of war…This is the purity of the universe as it was when it left the mighty hand of God'.

> At that moment, continues the author, the astronaut raised his eyes to look upon the most beautiful and amazing sight ever to burst upon the vision of man. Up from the sharp horizon of the moon rose the shining orb of Earth. He stood transfixed. His eye in a single moment swept from the snowcapped arctic to the snowcapped antarctic, with the oceans, the continents and the vast blanket of white glistening clouds in between…From this distance it looked as pure and beautiful and unstained as the moon upon which he stood. No sign of sin or greed or selfishness or violence could be seen….

Now, how would a preacher who is inspired by the Jewish ethic – which, as you know, does not believe in the doctrine of Original Sin – how would he describe this same experience? I believe he would do it in quite different terms. He would view the empty wastes of the moon not so much as unstained by any sin or vice but rather as wastes unsanctified by any virtue or noble deed. True, no lie has yet been told here; but, more to the point, neither has any truth ever been told or proclaimed in this lifeless world. Here, in these barren surroundings, no stone has ever borne witness to a feat of heroism or to an act of self-sacrifice, no site has been hallowed by prayer or love, and no grandeur of human creativity testifies to the partnership between God and His creatures in perfecting the universe He created.

Just as a glass half-filled with water strikes optimists as half-full and pessimists as half-empty, so do the same phenomena of an as yet incomplete world strike some for what man has achieved and others for what man has failed to accomplish. To the Jew, with his perennial optimism which assured his survival in the face of so much adversity, the brilliant orb of Earth far out beyond the moon's horizon would have induced a proud feeling of exhilaration, not a morbid mood of depression. He would behold it as the one planet in the vastness of space around him on which, transcending the strife and crime and vice plaguing it, countless generations have laboured to build a highly complex civilization, with its immortal triumphs of the human spirit, mind and heart, expressed in religion and literature, in art and science, in industry and social services.

Of course, he could not fail to see moral decadence abounding in our modern world. In the spurious name of progress, our permissive society has reincarnated the spirit of our antediluvian ancestors, with their loose morals, their caveman-like long hair and scant dresses, and even the wild erotic contortions of their primitive music.

But beneath these shifting sands of passing fads there is much solid rock of stability and fertile soil of creativity. The rates of divorce, of crime, of illegitimacy, of drug addiction may be alarming. Some students may delight in riots, some workers in reckless strikes, some employers in unethical exploitation, and some politicians in the abuse of power. But there are still countless homes which are happy and cheerful. The overwhelming majority of citizens are decent and law-abiding. Most children are born in wedlock, most students are responsible and eager to get on with their studies, most workers and employers are dedicated to their jobs, and – I dare say – most politicians are honest and concerned to promote the welfare of society.

True, on the world scene today, even if one does not look beyond the banner headlines of our newspapers, which read almost like a modern version of the Book of Job, we discover that mankind is tormented by many festering sores. All the major crisis-spots which afflicted the world a year ago continue unabated to bedevil human relations. The tragic conflicts in the Middle East, Vietnam, Biafra, Czechoslovakia and the racial strife in America have all persisted in wreaking terrible havoc during the past 12 months. To these travails have now been added the ominous Sino-Russian border clashes in the Far East and the frightening unrest in Northern Ireland in the Near West, with an assortment of riots and hijacks and kidnappings elsewhere thrown in for good measure. Judged by these criteria, the contemporary scene and future prospects on our planet look grim indeed.

And yet, from the distant perspective of a man on the moon, the human situation may appear entirely different. For every country at war or in the grip of terror there are dozens at peace. For every agitator plotting aggression or subversion there are hundreds of ordinary people who want to live in harmony with their neighbours. For every peddler of hate and mischief there are any number of decent folk who practise justice and kindness, who want to live and let live in security and happiness. Even inside the lands convulsed by strife and terror and oppression there are countless peace-loving citizens who harbour no evil against their neighbours. How many Russians, if they knew the full facts, would really desire to see Czech freedom brutally suppressed by military occupation, or their own Jewish fellow-citizens subjected to such heartless discrimination and repression? How many Irishmen want religious bigotry and social inequality driven to the brink of civil war? And how many Arabs among the hundred million ringing Israel really thirst for the annihilation of the Jewish State?

If only we used the tremendous amplifying machinery of our mass communications not to publicize the mischief of the few but rather to broadcast the pursuit of law and order and decency by the many, would not the human condition today look far less bleak and be more reassuring? Would not, as a result, the overwhelming majority of upright and peaceful people manage to contain and prevail over the relatively tiny minority of trouble-makers, agitators and warmongers? How much encouragement and strength would be given to our moral resources if only the press and TV cameras turned their spotlight on those of our youth who heroically resist temptation and defy the pressures of unchaste conformity instead of on those who affront human dignity by their shamelessness or cheap exhibitionism. The best defence against the spread of evil, as of any physical infection, lies in quarantine, in isolating it. Unfortunately, we do the opposite. In the hot competition for public attention in our news media, the advantage is always given to the noisy dissident over the quiet upholder of tradition, to the criminal over the law-abiding citizen, to the disturber of peace over the pursuer of peace, to the lustful beast in man over the disciplined best in man. In a ceaseless hunt for excitement serving to entertain, more befitting to the stage and fiction literature, our mass communications magnify the noise of violence and protest and obscenity, whilst muffling the voice of stability and moral sanity.

A personal experience the other day exemplifies this. Following the recent grievous fire at the Al-Aksa Mosque in Jerusalem, when the world press was full with blazing reports on the hysterical calls for a 'holy' war against Israel, I issued a public statement expressing the grief of the Jews in Britain over the damage done to one of Islam's holiest shrines. I appealed to responsible Arabs, and particularly to Muslim religious leaders, not to allow the disaster to be used as an instrument for fanning the flames of war and hatred, hoping that instead they would join us in the search and pursuit of a stable peace to assure the happiness of all peoples and the safety of all holy places in the region we commonly treasured as our national homes and birthplaces. But, alas, although I believe I expressed the yearning of far more people than did those who sought to whip up hatred and violence in the name of religion, the cry for war was more newsworthy and therefore widely publicized, while the plea for peace was all but ignored in the mass media.

Only last week Sir Peter Medawar, in a presidential address before the British Association for the Advancement of Science, justly decried the Prophets of gloom who blamed our science and technology for the deterioration of the world. We cannot but endorse his ringing challenge to those who surrendered their faith in human progress, although we may not altogether agree with his assertion that 'today we are conscious that human history is only just beginning. Only in the past 500 years have human beings begun to be, in the biological sense, a success.' We believe that the history of human civilization began when man first resolved to be God-like in making our earth different from the changeless sterility of the moon, and we believe that civilization will continue to advance so long as there are people yearning and working for a better world in which we rejoice in the happiness of our neighbours as in our own, placing mortal life into the service of immortal creations, knowledge into the service of moral and social advance, and the brotherhood of man into the service of our common Father. May the New Year find us worthy to be His partners in fashioning the world as He intended, a world in which, as our New Year liturgy has it, 'The just shall rejoice, the upright shall exult, and the pious shall be jubilant in song, when all wickedness shall be wholly consumed like smoke and the rule of arrogance shall pass away from the earth.'

3. The Meaning of Prayer and Confession*

During our forthcoming High Holydays (the New Year and the Day of Atonement) our Divine services in the synagogue will extend to a formidable total of some 25 hours. Even Jews who for the rest of the year are rather remote from religious observances will spend the greater part of this time in the house of prayer.

What do we hope to achieve during these long hours of devotion? Of course, we will pray, reciting many of our standard prayers over and over again; we will listen to numerous biblical passages, ranging from the sacrifice of Isaac to the exciting story of the prophet Jonah. We will be exhorted and uplifted by a number of edifying sermons, on themes and concepts stirring the Jewish conscience at the present time: our yearning for peace in the Holy Land, our anguish over the plight of Soviet Jewry, and our religious and moral responsibilities before God and man. And on the Day of Atonement we shall beat our hearts in contrite remorse, confessing our sins and failings during the past year.

But do we really need 25 hours – the better part of a working week – for these prayers, readings and exhortations? The question is all the more puzzling when we remember that often our

---

*New Year Broadcast, 1971

synagogue building programme is based on the requirement to contain the vast congregations expected for just these three days in the year.

To begin with, we must understand that the Jewish concept of prayer is quite distinct from the common meaning of the word. In the Jewish view, as the Hebrew term *lehitpalel* clearly implies, prayer is meant to *impress* rather than to *express* ourselves. God does not require to be informed of our wants and needs; He knows them better than we do. No, we pray and pour out our hearts before God for our own sake, to improve and ennoble ourselves by recognizing our own impotence and our dependence on our Maker, thus making ourselves worthy of the blessings for which we crave. It may take only minutes to *express* our desires, but it requires hours to change and regenerate ourselves through the *impression* of prayer.

Prayer and all other religious experiences, to be meaningful and effective, require first of all the creation of an atmosphere, a frame of mind, a spiritually responsive mood. Just as a blade of grass, even on the most fertile soil, cannot grow without air, sunshine and rain, so will the soul, or the human conscience, not blossom forth to its full potential unless it first be moved from the polluted environment of everyday existence to an atmosphere warmed by the sunshine of holiness, and refreshed by the rains of faith and rededication, borne on the clouds of inner turbulence and a genuinely distressed spirit.

It takes many hours of hard and sustained effort to produce such a mood. An hour's prayer a few times a year will no more moisten our hearts and cultivate our personality than a passing shower will irrigate a field; it takes days of sustained rain to make the earth yield its fruit.

Moreover, we believe that the necessary mood or environment cannot be created by an individual in isolation. It is a collective experience. It demands of the individual that he merge his identity within that of the community. In the Jewish view it is only as a group, as members of society, that we can effectively approach God and be truly roused by a religious experience. Hence our emphasis on public prayer; in fact, many of our most sacred prayers and readings require the quorum of a congregation and may not be recited in private.

Our Sages applied to public worship the biblical proverb: 'In the multitude of the people is the glory of the king.' The larger the congregation the greater the holiness of God, as it were – or, as we might say, the more can we appreciate His majesty and power, and the greater the resultant religious impact on the worshipper.

Let me develop this a little further and, by reference to a unique feature of Judaism, apply it to our own times. When we confess our sins, we do so neither as individuals nor through any priest or other intermediary. We list a whole catalogue of our failings collectively and directly before God. In our confession, we invariably speak in the plural: '*We* have sinned; *we* have been dishonest; *we* have slandered others; *we* have failed to honour father and mother.' Indeed, we mention, and seek forgiveness for, many offences – such as slander or robbery or even incest – which very few in the congregation are likely to have committed. But, if any one of us misconduct himself, we *all* have to plead guilty and seek atonement.

This is based on the cardinal Jewish doctrine that we are all accountable for one another. I am responsible for my neighbours, and they are responsible for me. According to our doctrine of Divine retribution, I will be punished not only for my own wrongs but for the wrongs of the community in which I live, just as the virtues and achievements of any individual bring credit and reward to all. Judaism therefore insists on cultivating not only the individual conscience, but the social conscience, to ensure a deep sense of collective responsibility.

The reason for this doctrine is quite simple. The first recorded question ever asked by man was: 'Am I my brother's keeper?' and the answer is: Yes, you certainly are! If anyone in our society defaults in his duties, shirks his obligations, each one of us is held responsible, for we all have a share in his guilt. We should have set a better example, or we should have prevented his misdeed by persuasion and argument, or we should have cared more about community service and the maintenance of law and order, of decency and moral rectitude. In one way or another, by acts of commission or omission, we all aid and abet in any crime, any vice found in our midst, and it is of no avail to plead: 'Why should I suffer for the sins of my neighbour?'

Few teachings of our faith have contributed more towards our people's triumph over the vicissitudes of our dispersion. Exiled from one country after another, we frequently had to make a fresh start as new immigrants, ever arriving as aliens on probation. In seeking to make ourselves acceptable and desirable, we were greatly helped by the deeply ingrained feeling of collective responsibility, the awareness that the misconduct of any individual brought the entire community into disrepute. By making every Jew feel that, in committing an offence, he would disgrace not only himself and his family, but his entire people, this sense of collective guilt served as a most powerful deterrent to individual aberrations, amounting in effect to communal sanctions against any delinquents. Any Jew contemplating an illegal or ignoble act knew that he would incur the community's wrath and denunciation for tarnishing the good name of all. Consequently, he would think twice before committing such an act.

By the same token, the corporate social conscience served as an effective incentive to encourage public service and deeds of distinction. The corollary to collective guilt is collective honour, whereby anyone distinguishing himself enables all to share in his glory – an extra inducement to foster acts of outstanding value and service.

This highly developed sense of corporate shame and corporate honour, as a deterrent to vice and an incentive to virtue, clearly proved an important factor in ensuring a notably low rate of crime and fostering a correspondingly high rate of enduring services to humanity, as indicated by the disproportionate number of Jews among Nobel prize winners.

In our shrinking world of instant communication and growing interdependence, the call for collective responsibility is now a major universal challenge. We can no longer isolate the welfare or the ordeals of a country, or of individuals, from the rest of humanity. For the war in far-away Vietnam, or racial discrimination in distant South Africa, or the Arab–Israel conflict, or the trans-Atlantic jitters of the once almighty dollar, bring crisis, turmoil, agitation and insecurity to the whole world. Yet we suffer from such a surfeit of disasters, that we are seldom personally affected by even the most colossal calamities, How many of us really care about the unspeakable horrors suffered in Bengal through the havoc wrought by a frightful civil war compounded by unprecedented floods engulfing millions? Even nearer home, we tend to be hardened to insensitivity by the constant reports on terror in Northern Ireland, stories of violence in our streets, and instances of moral erosion among our youth. When a policeman is gunned down, or when crazy gangs of young people set out on a frenzy of vandalism, or when, less sensationally, countless marriages break up in misery poisoned by the pollution of pornography, or when nearly a million of our fellow citizens are condemned by unemployment to the misery of want and the indignity of idleness, how many really care?

But in what way can we *all* be held responsible for these evils and how can we prevent them? Let me illustrate the answer by just one or two examples. Just as the flowers of virtue, like the inspiration of prayer, flourish only in a clean atmosphere charged with moral fervour, so do the weeds of evil proliferate in a sick society, muddied by blatant immorality. Violence and agitation breed on publicity and notoriety. We all help in promoting such publicity. If people did not enjoy reading sordid stories of crime, cruelty and the antics of the irresponsibles of society, our newspapers and magazines would not feature them so prominently. They would concentrate on reporting man's successes and not headlining his failures. Similarly, if decent people were outraged with revulsion rather than bored, let alone titillated, by erotic displays and lurid accounts of divorces and adultery, the murky sources of smut and faithlessness would the sooner be cleaned up.

We hear much criticism these days of the silent majority. Although I am not sure that a majority can be anything but relatively silent, nevertheless it should not passively connive at evil by tolerating it or failing to strengthen the defences against it. To preserve law and order is not just the business of policemen; it is the business of every citizen to report crime when he sees it and to extend a helping hand to the victim of violence when he witnesses it. To preach decency and uprightness is not just the business of priests or rabbis; to engage in social welfare is not just the task of social workers, and to instruct our children in morality is not simply the exclusive prerogative of professional teachers; every human owes it to society to reprove others guilty of wrongdoing, to give up some of his time for community service, and to teach his children the difference between right and wrong. If the individual defaults in any of these obligations, he is accountable for the consequences. Even in government and politics, it is ultimately only the concern and the participation of all citizens that can avoid chaos and moral decline. A discriminating electorate ensures discriminating politicians; and a judicious citizenry produces judicious teachers, journalists, scientists, artists and other pace-setters of our community.

I referred earlier to the story of Jonah, our final biblical reading during the solemn Days of Awe ahead of us. Does this story not dramatize our theme on the predicament of the world today and the responsibility of every individual in it? Here we see a prophet of God foiled by disaster in his attempt to flee from his mission and forced to return to his assignment. Here we see the lives of an entire ship's company first threatened and then saved because of the actions of a single individual among them. And here we see a vast city, in which evil was rampant, doomed to destruction and later reprieved. However few the actual criminals, all citizens were held accountable for the city's degeneration, and it was the sincere repentance of the entire population, prodded by the call of just one individual, that finally saved the city.

Today, in our shrunken world, we are all in the same boat; anyone escaping from his mission and shirking his responsibilities endangers us all. Today, moreover, the whole world is one vast Niniveh, corrupted by evil and oppression, and threatened with the doom of chaos, strife and lawlessness.

As we gather in our synagogues to seek the blessings of a New Year on behalf of all our fellow-men, a call goes forth as it did to the inhabitants of Niniveh: Let every man and woman, from the greatest to the smallest, 'cry mightily unto God; yea, let them turn every one from his evil way and from the violence that is in their hands. Who knows whether God will not turn and repent, and turn away from his fierce anger, that we perish not?' May we each help to make all worthy of the gifts of life, health and happiness in a year destined, we pray, to bring to the world abundant peace, universal freedom and prosperity for all humans.